HOLIDAY FOLKLORE, PHOBIAS and FUN

Mythical Origins, Scientific Treatments and Superstitious "Cures"

Other Outcomes Unlimited books and products by Dr. Dossey:

Books:

Keying: The Power of Positive Feelings:
Overcoming Fears, Phobias and Stress, 1989.

Psychological Aftershock:
What To Do Before, During and After Any Disaster, Forthcoming.

Audio cassettes:

THROUGH THE BRIAR PATCH:
 Your Complete Personal Power Program, 1987

PREDICTABLE COMMUNICATION STRATEGIES, 1985

FRIDAY THE 13TH, 1988

MAKE RESOLUTIONS WORK, 1988

KEYING: THE POWER OF POSITIVE FEELINGS, 1990

HOLIDAY FOLKLORE, PHOBIAS and FUN

Mythical Origins,
Scientific Treatments and
Superstitious "Cures"

By
Donald E. Dossey, Ph.D.

1992
Outcomes Unlimited Press, Inc.
Los Angeles, CA, 90024, U.S.A.

HOLIDAY FOLKLORE, PHOBIAS and FUN: Mythical Origins,
Scientific Treatments and Superstitious "Cures"

Outcomes Unlimited Press, Inc., Publisher
1015 Gayley Avenue, Ste.1165
Los Angeles, California 90024

Graphic Business Systems, Typographers
Redondo Beach, California

McNaughton & Gunn, Inc., Lithographers
Ann Arbor, Michigan

Cover and Artwork by
Lois Erickson, C. Carrington and Cindra Shields

Library of Congress Cataloging-in-Publication Data

Dossey, Donald E., 1934-
    Holiday folklore, phobias, and fun: mythical origins, scientific
treatments, and superstitious "cures" / by Donald E. Dossey
        p.   cm.
    Includes bibliographical references and index.
    ISBN Number: 0-925640-06-9 (hard) : $18.95
    ISBN Number: 0-925640-07-7 (soft) : $14.95
    1. Holidays--Folklore. 2. Holidays--United States. 3.Phobias--Popular works.
4. Neurolinguistic programming--Popular works.
I. Title.
GR930.D67 1992
398'.33--dc20   92-2467
                                                                      CIP

DEDICATION
To Lois, my dearest love and soul-mate, for helping me in overcoming the fears of commitment and teaching me the difference between the true love of God and the superstitious dreams of this world.

HOLIDAY FOLKLORE, PHOBIAS and FUN

Mythical Origins, Scientific Treatments and Superstitious "Cures"

TABLE OF CONTENTS

ACKNOWLEDGEMENTS

Thanks to the many radio and television talk show hosts and producers for the contributions they have made to this book. Especially Paul Gonzales and Ray Appleton who were particularly instrumental in encouraging me to write it. Even though I have never met Edna Barth, to her goes an enormous amount of thanks and deep, deep gratitude. Her wonderful children's books on the folklore of various holidays were my original source of inspiration for these media appearances, and have been used amply in this book.

My deepest gratitude to Lois Erickson for her loving support and editorial skills without which I would have been unable to write this book. I want to acknowledge my understanding mother, Elsie, for making it possible at all. Thanks to Ed and Addie Ostrowski, Fran and Bob Ulrich, Jenny and Al Asher, my brother Vic Dossey, my sister-in-law Kay Nelson Dossey, Elaine Demond and Don Giesbrecht for their input and taking the time to listen to me, time and time again, agonizing over a title. Fran, Bob and Addie need a special note; Addie for being my long-distant editor and grammarian, and Fran and Bob for their suggestions from the book's beginnings.

My appreciation also extends to Nancy Compton at McNaughton and Gunn for teaching me what I needed to know about printing, Cindra Shields, my wonderful daughter and owner of Graphic Business Systems, for her helpful hints and typesetting, Aaron Silverman at SCB Distributors who keeps me on the ground and Steven Hall, editor and owner of Radio and TV Reports, for his contribution and encouragement.

Howard Geer, my deep friend, and Maria Sanchez are special kinds of publicists.

Thank you all.

PREFACE

Holiday Folklore, Phobias and Fun: Mythical Origins, Scientific Treatments and Superstitious "Cures" is not simply an entertaining book about ancient beginnings of our holiday customs, but also contains a complete scientific guide to overcoming the anxieties and phobias surrounding our holidays.

The rising curiosity about the captivating folklore that surrounds our holiday customs is more than satisfied as this enchanting book delves into the intriguing origins of holiday legends and symbols. With each fascinating chapter, you will be intrigued with unusual, often hilarious, ancient magical folklore "cures" for superstitions and fears.

This bewitching book explores the time when magic was science and superstition was religion in a tongue-in-cheek fashion that has never been done before.

It probes, often humorously, the enticing and gripping little known legends of Celtic customs, Greek and Roman historical and mythical superstitions as well as current supernatural practices.

Many a curious person has asked, "Dr. Dossey, how did a phobia specialist and an expert witness on Anxiety Disorders and Post-traumatic Stress Disorders get interested in the folklore origins and superstitions that surround our holidays?" The answer is somewhat curious.

For more than 10 years I have been interviewed on various radio and television shows and news broadcasts worldwide discussing the results of curing anxiety, phobias and stress while directing the Phobia Institute and Stress Management Centers of Southern California.

Numerous national and international newspapers and magazines have published the findings from my earlier book, *Keying: The Power of Positive Feelings: Overcoming Fears, Phobias and Stress.* They were particularly interested in the Keying technique, a process that predictably and measurably helps people wash away anxieties, phobias, post-traumatic stress and stress related disorders.

Not a small number of people had been calling, on various occasions, for treatment of problems relating to the holidays or concerned about having specific fears just before, during and, often, immediately following certain holidays.

Around Halloween, for example, some had symptoms that ranged from mild anxiety to extreme fear while others had full blown phobias and panic attacks.

Others suffered from excruciatingly fearful symptoms prior to and on the day and date of Friday the 13th which I named as "paraskevidekatriaphobia," the fear of Friday the 13th. I tell my patients, "When you learn to pronounce it, you're cured!"

Still others would call complaining of anxiety and fearful feelings, and, often, obsessive compulsive behaviors prior to or on St. Valentine's Day.

Some would begin to have horrible symptoms of anxiety and phobias beginning around Thanksgiving, going through and including Christmas or Hanukkah, and lasting for some two or three weeks after New Year's Day. That particular phenomenon has been labeled "The Holiday Blues."

And so it went throughout the year. It was found that millions of people suffer from extraordinary anxiety and stress on, or near, major holidays and certain other times like vacations or back to school months.

Now, I knew that all of us have various pestering thoughts and nagging feelings around certain holidays or days, like Friday the 13th or April Fool's Day, but not to such an extent as to have to call a phobia or stress clinic or to call me on a radio or television show, as many did, to discuss them or to otherwise seek help.

I was struck with curiosity. "Why," I thought, "would a person acquire symptoms of anxiety or a phobia around certain holidays or events and not get anxious or fearful around others?"

I started researching our various holiday customs, their ancient folklore, and mythical origins and superstitions, hoping to see if therein could be the cause of some people becoming phobic or anxious, or why some exhibited maladaptive behavior, around certain holidays or specific times of the year.

I was assuming that, armed with that kind of information, I could help my patients more effectively overcome their anxiety and stress. The results? It didn't help at all. No matter how much information I gave them about the holiday around which they had a problem, they didn't get any better, their symptoms weren't diminished one iota.

They were like persons who had had automobile accidents. They had all kinds of information, they knew why they had the phobia, and yet they were still afraid of driving. That kind of understanding is fascinating and interesting, but it is worthless, I found, when it comes to curing anxiety disorders and phobias.

But, all was not lost because, as I said, I ended up with a lot of information about the various holiday customs and their folklore.

I was overwhelmed at the interest and fascination of the media in my findings. I also found that reporting on the data was a new and exciting gateway through which to better acquaint people with my first book.

Then, on one particular Friday the 13th, I was being interviewed by one of the best talk show hosts with whom I have ever worked, Ray Appleton. He humorously, and out of the blue, introduced me as the great "folklorian historian." It was on that day that Ray asked me if I had ever thought of writing a book on the subject of holiday folklore and phobias. He was afraid that the information was on its way to being dangerously and unforgivably lost forever.

I didn't take him too seriously at the time, but not more than a month later I received numerous requests from radio and television talk show hosts, and one newspaper editor, asking me to do a program on April Fools' Day folklore and superstitions. I had never done any research on April Fools' Day origins, but realized that I had created a reputation of supposedly knowing about folklore surrounding all of our holidays.

Rather than admitting ignorance, I called one of my closest friends, Jenny Asher, and asked her to read me what her encyclopedia had to say about April Fools' Day origins. I, then, looked up more information at the reference desk at the local library. Now I had enough information to do the shows. It suddenly dawned on me that Ray was right, I should write the book.

Thus began my second career as a "folklorian historian." From then on I began seriously researching holiday folklore and phobias, mythical origins, magical spells and superstitious "cures." Hence, the name of the book: *Holiday Folklore, Phobias and Fun: Mythical Origins, Scientific Treatments and Superstitious "Cures"*

I have found that many people are both fascinated and terrorized by the holidays. There is a fine line between folklore and phobias. For some it becomes difficult to distinguish the folklore of hobgoblins, pumpkins and fun from the black magic, voodoo and fearful superstitions that move us one step beyond into the areas of dangerous rituals and harmful fears and phobias.

This book hurdles the chasm between folklore and science. It contains an unusual and informative list of fears and phobias from which millions of people suffer, and a complete system for handling anxieties and stress.

Whether you have anxieties surrounding a particular holiday or you are simply curious about the secrets and little known facts about our holiday customs and humorous superstitious "cures," you will find this guidebook invaluable.

INTRODUCTION

HAVE YOU EVER WONDERED...

... why we make New Years resolutions?

... how Cupid, hearts, love birds and red roses became associated with Valentine's Day?

... who St. Patrick was and what his day has to do with leprechauns?

... if you suffer from "paraskevidekatriaphobia," or why Friday the 13th was chosen as the "bad" day and not Monday the 11th?

... where the bunny rabbit, eggs and other symbols of Easter originated?

... how pranks and tricks got associated with April Fools' Day?

... why Halloween witches ride brooms instead of magic carpets, how the jack-o-lantern was named or if goblins really existed?

... what the true source of our Thanksgiving celebration is?

... where the custom of kissing under the mistletoe came from and why holly is a part of Christmas?

... why crossing black cats' paths, stepping on cracks and spilling salt, etc. have been unlucky for centuries?

... if it is better to hang all of your socks with holes in them outside your window to ward off the evil spirits or chew a piece of beef gristle while standing on your head?

... what present-day techniques can help you overcome any phobia or holiday stress?

Centuries pass, holidays come and go, and, for many of us, the origins of the ancient customs are only vague memories or have been lost completely.

Few girls dancing around a maypole are aware that they are paying tribute to the reproductive powers of the phallus; few people having a drink at an office or factory Christmas party know that they are repeating an age-old ritual of attempting to be transformed by the powers of the liquor in order to assist in transforming the barren landscape of winter to fertile, life-giving spring; and few, if any, realize that blowing horns, ringing bells and shouting on New Year's Eve was also used by our ancient ancestors to frighten away any evil spirits that may have been present. Yet, year after year, most of us continue to perform such holiday rituals by rote, participating in holiday customs and using symbols that, in many cases, have been in existence for 2,000 to 10,000 years.

I know I may sound a little "cracked" to consider some of what I am saying, but it is like my dear friend, Al Asher, once told me, "It's good to be somewhat cracked, Donald, because that lets a little light in."

Hopefully, this book will remind us of our long-forgotten holiday history. However, how do you sort out all of the available information and then funnel your selections that make sense into the relatively few pages of a book without hurting someone by leaving out information, or, possibly, not interpreting the findings exactly the way one particular scholar thinks you should?

The only obvious answer is that this is not intended to be an exhaustive work, but simply an arbitrary selection of holiday folklore and phobias, their mythical origins, magical spells and superstitious "cures."

This book belongs to no "school" of folklore, adheres to no "method," advocates no "theory." I have not intentionally left out any folklore or legends, nor included any with any conscious bias or prejudice. Those included are only the selected ones that appeared to fit in the intended framework of information, intrigue, fun and light-heartedness. Accuracy is intended, but not guaranteed. Hopefully, I have exhibited good taste and stayed within the parameters of the scholar while helping in some small way to save part of the essence of our great heritage of western civilization.

Whether we like it or not, not just a few of the so-called pagan celebrations and customs have been assigned Christian meaning.

Many of the primitive rituals have prevailed throughout our holiday customs and have not diluted one iota of the Christian significance of spirituality and religiosity. Perhaps, with an open eye, we may be able to see that these customs have even enhanced our mystical and spiritual experience.

Hopefully this book will help to dispel the myths that have created fear and misery in the world, to put some illumination on our great inheritance, and to lighten up, with a more humorous point of view, our endowment from our ancestors.

My purpose is not to put illegitimate or unverifiable voodoo into our holidays. It is, however, my sincere attempt to restore their rightful curious enchantment and genuine magic.

An attempt has been earnestly made to help remind us of some of the possible "forgotten" folklore, mythical origins, symbols and superstitions encircling the various holiday customs. And, with a tongue-in-cheek approach, help us to remember some of the assorted omens, predictions, spells and "cures" associated with them.

Each chapter will start out with basic folklore facts that you will often see overlap into other holidays. It is fun to discover the same mythical characters and themes as they reappear throughout the year's special celebrations.

Many of the legendary Rx's, spells and folklore "cures" also often overlap and are somewhat generic. That is, frequently one can be used for good luck in general and at other times the same ritual can be applied specifically to attain financial abundance or good health. Many of these have multiple sources which, if listed, would be too distracting to the reader. Please refer to the Bibliography for more specific information.

An acknowledgement and a note of endorsement should be made to the animal lovers of the world. In no way is this book suggesting that animals, or parts thereof, be used for magical spells and sacrificial rites. Any mention of them is historical and in the framework of amusement, lightheartedness and fun.

Included in each chapter are the more common phobias, stresses and anxieties surrounding the annual festivities along with some up-to-date suggestions on how to handle them a little more easily. A partial sampling of the statistics is staggering. It has been estimated that...

60 million believe in witches,

35 million people have wiccaphobia, the fear of witches,

25 million have reported seeing the devil,

45 million people have demophobia, the fear of demons,

80 million people in the USA have had an ESP experience,

159 million (90%) of the population suffer from some form of the "holiday blues," and

17 million suffer from paraskevidekatriaphobia, the fear of Friday the 13th.

Various chapters include scientific methods of curing any phobia or stress disorder. When combined, the suggestions contain the three major legs of the tripod supporting a systematic, easy, safe and predictable system to better control the feelings, thoughts and actions that cause problems. The tripod consists of taking command of the mind, mastering the physical feelings and controlling the actions that may get in the way of happiness, perfect health, success and peace of mind... especially the angst and stress that occur around the holidays.

An attempt has been made to remove the superstitions surrounding psychiatry and psychotherapy in terms of their effectiveness and how they are chosen for the practice of mental health therapy. The research strongly suggests that because of the lack of substantiated positive results, one could advance the case that they call their business a "private practice" because practicing and rehearsing appears to be what they're best at.

Also, a look is taken at the similarities of the ancient shamans and witch doctors of other cultures to the present-day psychologists and psychotherapists. Research has shown that the rituals, incantations and physical practices are amazingly similar. How the Bushmen of Alaska train their schizophrenic children to be witch doctors, their wise men of the tribe, is another parallel with our current psychotherapists, except our selection process is not as obvious as theirs. Rumor has it that the Bushmen's methods may be more effective.

Chapter X is a quasi-alphabetical listing of various common, and not so common, folklore superstitions not falling into any specific category or holiday. It catalogs superstitions, folklore remedies, "magical" spells and "cures" such as why we throw spilled salt over our shoulder, how crossing a black cat's path became bad luck, why we throw rice all over the bride and groom at a wedding and what our ancestors were up to when they hung horseshoes over their heads.

The Appendixes contain holiday recipes, additional scientific tips on handling anxiety and stress, and the Fear and Phobia Finder which comprises of a list of over 250 phobias. The Index is a complete cross-reference of folklore, phobias and superstitions.

The Bibliography and suggested readings do not reflect the information I gathered while being a guest on numerous radio and television shows throughout the world. While discussing folklore, phobias, superstitious remedies and magical spells, I learned many that were not in the books. Some sources were quite academic and some were not, but I wanted to show the flavor of the wonderful heritage upon which our great culture stands.

As we all know, bats have almost always been considered evil omens in much of our ancient folklore. However, if you really want to get "batty" and have people think you may have "bats in your belfry," look at how bats can bring good fortune to you.

Not only the well known, "Bat, bat come under my hat" that could bring very good luck, but also, if you need hair, a bat's heart has been considered excellent for curing baldness.

Have trouble with ants? Wings of a bat placed on an ant hill will prevent the ants from coming out, according to one medieval writer.

If you like to gamble, here is an old Mississippi divination trick. Cut the heart from a live bat and tie it to the right wrist where it can not be seen. This will bring good luck to the gambler.

And if things get a little too hectic and you want to hide out for a while, or go to the Bahamas and escape, obtain the eye of a bat. That, according to ancient folklore, will make the owner invisible.

I hope you enjoy the book.

NEW YEAR'S DAY - PART I

MYTHICAL ORIGIN, FOLKLORE OMENS AND PREDICTIONS

HAVE YOU EVER WONDERED...

... why we celebrate New Year's Day?

... when the first known celebration took place?

... what some of the many pagan vestiges associated with New Year's are?

... where the customs of wearing masks, ringing bells and excessive high-spirited noisemaking on New Year's Eve come from?

... why we clink glasses together when making a toast?

... why we celebrate New Year's Day on January 1 instead of March 25 like we used to?

... why people make New Year's Resolutions?

... why New Year's resolutions are such notorious failures?

... if it is possible to become addicted to unhappiness, failure and negative habits?

... why phrases like "I won't procrastinate anymore," and "I will stop eating candy bars," don't work?

... what the best way is to formulate New Year's Resolutions to increase the chances for their success?

... if the well known Keying process helps people change habits a lot more easily? If it can better our health?

... what De-briefing is and why it is so important?

... what specific Refocusing techniques a person can use?

... if my motto, "You can always have a good day!" is really a true possibility?

NEW YEAR'S FOLKLORE

The transitions from the old to the new, with their associated rituals, are observed in as many different ways as there are peoples in the world. The one universal thing they all share is the notion that these *rites de passage* are commemorating one sequence of life as ended and another as unfolding.

Birth, entering adulthood, marriage, fertility rites and death all fall into this category. So do hazing in college and the dubbing of a knight. And the remembrance of events, such as birthdays and anniversaries, are celebrated in all cultures.

These *rites de passage* are defined in *Funk & Wagnalls' Standard Dictionary of Folklore, Mythology and Legend,* as ceremonies which usher an individual,or group,into a new way of life or new status in life. The feeling tone of each person or group is a key factor in determining whether its response will be one of regret, joy or hope. New Year's Day is a case in point.

Historically, New Year's Day has always been problematic. Merely deciding when it was to be has not been easy. The first known New Year's celebration took place in Mesopotamia in 2000 B.C., when the year began with the new moon closest to either the spring or the autumn equinox, depending on where you happened to live.

In early Europe, New Year's Day occurred on various dates, including March and Christmas, regardless of the Roman reforms. The Greeks, the Chinese and the Jews disagreed with this timetable, but no one suggested that the year commence on January 1, according to Jane Hatch in *The American Book of Days*, until the Romans got the idea in 153 B.C.

Julius Caesar, in 45 B.C., revised the calendar and reinstituted January as the first month in what was called the *Julian Calendar*. It followed immediately after the festival of *Saturnalia*, a period of fertility rites, the wearing of masks, noisemaking and great rejoicing. The observances were for the purpose of increasing the fruitfulness of nature and the people and to ensure the turning of the sun northward again. The wearing of masks was to chase away evil spirits or for hiding from them. The ringing of bells was used for the same purpose. (See Chapter VII on Halloween for more on bells and masks).

The Romans also traditionally celebrated the Feast of Janus (thus the name for our month, January). Hatch says that Janus is "the god of doorways and of beginnings, who is depicted as looking both forward to the future and backward to the past." On the first of January gifts of "strength," after the goddess *Strenia,* and optimism were exchanged. *Stranae* is also Latin for "omens" and we can begin to see the semantic connections with our present-day superstitions and the anticipation with which we great the New Year.

The Christians opposed, deplored and condemned this day, and its practices, as diabolical. The Council of Tours required prayers and a mass of repentance on New Year's Day, which it said was "a practice long in use." Fasts were required as penance for sins, and dances were forbidden.

The innovation of having New Year's Day fall on January 1 caught on slowly. In early medieval times, most of Europe felt the year began on March 25 (the Feast of the Annunciation, also known as Lady Day). The English started their new year on Christmas Day, until William the Conqueror shifted it to January 1. In 1155, England changed the rules again —- back to Lady Day —- and for the next 427 years, March 25 was the first day of the year.

In 1582, however, Pope Gregory XIII restored it to its former glory, January 1. Except for Russia, most of the European Catholic countries immediately embraced the idea. Protestant nations, a cantankerous lot, balked, and some did not switch for two centuries; Scotland in 1600, and England in 1752. (See April Fool's Day and why these die-hards were called the "fools".) Thus the celebration of January 1 as the first day of the year is a modern innovation.

The excessive, vigorous, high-spiritedness which characterizes the New Year, however, cannot be attributed solely to the Roman festivals of Saturnalia and Janus.

Some credit is due certain other peoples. In pre-Christian times, for example, the Celtic Druids, and later the invading Saxons, performed celebrations and rituals to induce the gods of fertility to smile upon their crops and women in the coming new year. Exchanging gifts was also practiced by most Europeans until the practice died out around the mid-19th century.

It is well to note that with practically all ancient rituals for every celebration, and many *rites of passage*, we find fertility rites the most important aspect of our early ancestors' life. That is, the need for human procreation, plentiful crops and healthy animals was uppermost in their minds.

We have our New Year's rituals to be sure, but many other cultures have customs so specific that they make our observances seem noncommittal. In Thailand for instance, friends throw water on each other when they meet.

In Japan, the entrance to a house must be hung with a *shimenawa* (a rope made of rice straw) to banish evil spirits, and decorated with ferns, bitter orange and lobster to purify the household of evil. They offer the sun a "male" cake and the moon, of course, a "female" cake.

Some Moslems in northern Africa light bonfires and leap over them. The highlight of the Tamil New Year's festivities in southern India is the ritual boiling of the *new rice*, an act with an excitement level that might remind some of a bowl of Mexican jumping beans.

Other cultures also consider the ending of one year and the beginning of the next as a moment of gratification. *Funk and Wagnalls* says that "In China, the first few days of the new year are the only days celebrated as universal festivals. All shops are customarily closed, and the lowest coolie then takes his annual leave to be with his family for a few days." The household gods return to join the reunion, having completed their various duties.

Proverbs are posted to chase away evil spirits and welcome the gods of wealth and babies to their home. The head of the house relaxes and makes plans for the new year only after paying all of his debts before midnight. (A practice the Federal government should consider in its budgetary affairs.)

In both Japan and China, New Year's Day is everybody's birthday.

Much excitement is created in Bengal with the congregating of tens of thousands of people in the waters of the Ganges river, which they worship. In Ceylon, rice cakes are offered by the Veddas. The Persian New Year, which eventually became the Moslem New Year, is when, it is believed, Solomon received his ring back from God, gifts from the devil, and water that was sprinkled on him by swallows.

Cakes made in the form of a boar from the first sheaf, are used in some northern European countries. In France, pancakes are cooked on a griddle to bring good luck and riches.

The Scots celebrate Hogmanay with masked children who go about singing and soliciting oat cakes on the last day of the old year. Some scholars believe this is an echo of the times when the ancient Druids, on the last day of the year, gathered mistletoe. This tends to show our historical continuity and common bond even more than we might expect.

North American Indian groups also have rites to greet the new year, though not always at the same time of year.

An Iroquois group, the Senecas, observes 7-8 days of rites which include the creation of "new fire," masquerading, interpretation of dreams, confession of sins, songs and offerings.

The Northwest California Indians and the Hopi Indians have New Year ceremonies that are more dedicated to initiating the young men into the tribe during what they call the *Wuwuchim*.

Several American Indian tribes have formed what is called the World Renewal cult. Its ceremonies are practiced to venerate the earth, the first-fruits and the "new fire," thus preventing illness and trouble for one more year.

New Year's in the United States occurs midway between Christmas and Epiphany (January 6), and not including Christmas itself, is the most celebrated of festivities during this joyous season. And with it come many pagan vestiges; the honoring of evergreens, the yule log burning, and the lighting of the "new fire." Coffin and Cohen go on to say that the "indulgence in sexual license and intoxicating drink, processions of mummers and maskers, ritualistic combat between opposing parties, and the pledging of good resolves in order to redeem the bad behavior of the past."

According to *Funk and Wagnalls*, "Many Occidental countries mark the passing of the old year and the arrival of the new by elaborate balls, drinking, and generally orgiastic behavior in which, at midnight, everybody blows horns, rings bells, shouts, throws confetti, sings 'Should old acquaintance be forgot,' drinks additional toasts which are usually not needed, and, as an important part of the ritual, tries to kiss all the prettiest girls in the party, who offer enthusiastic collaboration."

Yes, we still have our ritualistic parties, parades and sports events. We have New York's Times Square, the Philadelphia Mummers Parade, Pasadena's Tournament of Roses, the Pennsylvania's Fantasticals, Ed McMahon, Dick Clark (whose never-changing appearance casts doubt on the whole passage-of-time concept), indigestion and, in general, the ever ominous New Year's resolutions.

Let us not exclude, of course, the fact that this is the day to celebrate American patriot Paul Revere's birthday, and is the anniversary of President Lincoln's final Emancipation Proclamation, an event which earned it the title of Emancipation Day.

LET US NOT LEAP OVER LEAP YEAR

The first Leap Year recorded dates back to 45 B.C. when Julius Caesar reformed the calendar. His new *Julian calendar* included an an extra day every fourth year. This still did not work out too well because it did not align with the seasons, and the fact that the earth's rotation around the sun is 365 days, five hours, 48 minutes and a little more that 45 seconds. Pope Gregory XIII remedied the situation in 1582 by changing the Old Style calendar to the the New Style calendar which we use today. He kept February 29 to be added every fourth year. In doing so, he brought it closely in line with the astronomical year, off by only 26 seconds a year.

Why we use the term *Leap Year* is actually not known, but the general consensus of scholars is that it had to do with how it was perceived in the eyes of the law. Early on, this extra day was not considered as "legal" in the courts, so February 29 was missed, skipped or "leaped over."

Why it is the day for unmarried women to propose to available men is also a mystery. Some believe it began with an old Irish legend about St. Patrick and St. Bridget. Bridget, it is told, was unhappy because her nuns could not propose to men and protested to Patrick (marriage was allowed at that time for the clergy). After a series of negotiations, Patrick agreed to let the women have the privilege of proposing to men every Leap Year. Shortly after that, Bridget proposed to Patrick! He turned her down, but instead he promised her a kiss and a silk gown.

It became unwritten law by the Middle Ages that any man who refused a proposal from a woman on Leap Year was required to pay with a kiss, and a pair of gloves or a silk dress.

In 1288, it became law in Scotland and men who refused were fined up to one pound. The only way out of paying, by law, was to pretend that he was engaged to her or make it appear that he agreed to the proposal.

By the 15th century, it had also become law in parts of Europe and eventually came to the United States. Here, we do not take the custom quite that seriously...unless there is an old unknown law that is still on the books. So beware, men, and if you are concerned, check with your state authorities.

OMENS, RITUALS AND PREDICTIONS

Put a dime under your plate on New Year's Day and be happy, wealthy and healthy all year long.

Wear red garters to bring you good luck. The ancient source did not state whether this was for women only. Use your own judgment.

It is considered bad luck to hang a new calendar or almanac before daylight on New Year's Day, so says Ferne Shelton in her collections *Pioneer Superstitions: Old-Timey Signs and Sayings.*

If, on New Year's Day, a man enters the house first, you can look forward to good luck the rest of the year. However, if a woman comes in first, expect bad luck. So, do as Mrs. M.T. Faye of Tennessee did. She hired a man to come to the house and go into every room before she would cook breakfast. However, expect a late breakfast.

If a woman comes to see you on New Year's Day, the chickens will all be pullets; if a man comes, they will all be roosters.

If you sew on New Year's Day, you will sew a shroud before the year is out.

Always wear something new on New Year's Day for good luck during the year.

If you cry on New Year's Day, you will be sorry throughout the year.

What you do the first hour of the New Year will be what you do most of the year. So, do not do anything on New Year's that you don't wish to do all year.

You can figure on bad luck if you take anything out of the house on January 1st according to Cohen and Coffin in *The Folklore of American Holidays.*

For good luck, each person entering a house on January 1st must bring something (anything) in. This is an echo of the ancient gift-bearing customs practiced on this day.

If you have many visitors on this day you will have many more to come during the year.

To overcome procrastination, a person must do something worthwhile this day, or he might "be idle and piddling all year."

However, if you do not want hard work all year, stay away from the washing machine and do not wash clothes this day.

Another one says that if you wash your clothes on New Year's Day, you will wash someone out of your family. (This may be an omen or a ritual. It depends upon your desired outcome!)

Bad luck will befall you if you sweep the house on New Year's Day.

Go to all the windows of your house and open them for a few minutes just before midnight on New Year's Eve. This lets the "bad luck out and the good luck in" for the coming year.

To prevent fits, hang a bag of peony seeds around your neck.

Babies born on New Year's Day will always be lucky.

Men should do most of the work on New Year's Eve to bring good luck.

Luck will go away if you open the front door.

A legendary explanation for clinking glasses is that the intention of the clink was to produce a bell-like noise to banish evil spirits and the devil.

Wassail bowls in wealthy homes were provided for the poor to toast "To your health!" "Wassailing" was practiced by the poor, or by the excessive drinker, to get their share of the libations. (See also, Christmas folklore.)

RECIPES FOR PROSPERITY AND ABUNDANCE

For a prosperous year, cook something on New Year's Day that swells.

Eat turnip greens, hog jowls, blackeyed peas, cabbage and peaches on New Year's day to bring luck, health and wealth during the year.

Eat collard greens on New Year's to have paper money all year.

If you cook and eat specifically blackeyed peas and hog head on New Year's Day, you'll have plenty to eat the rest of the year.

If people eat sauerkraut on New Year's Day they will become rich.

Money cooked in blackeyed peas on New Year's means you will have money all year.

Pennsylvanians suggest you eat turkey on Christmas and pork with sauerkraut on New Year's Day. Why? Because pork symbolizes the "forward look" of the turn of the year. A fowl scratches backward—a pig roots forward.

An old German belief was that if you kept cabbage or herring in the house on New Year's Eve, you will have money all year. And if you eat a piece of herring at the stroke of midnight, you will be lucky all year long.

Do not make or break any contract on the First.

To run out of salt on New Year's Day means poverty all year. So always make sure the salt-shaker is full on New Year's Day, and then you will prosper throughout the year.

RECIPES FOR GOOD LUCK AND HEALTH

Eat black-eyed pea soup on January 1st to bring happiness and health throughout the year. According to Cindra Shields, my lovely daughter, it is called Hoppin' John Soup.

To have good luck all the year, eat a piece of boiled meat on the first day of January.

Rice and peas on New Year's Day bring good luck.

Eat cabbage and pork sausage on January 1st.

Eat sauerkraut on New Year's Day to keep well the rest of the year.

For New Year's, lobster represents good health and happiness. If you drop it, get a new one, otherwise bad luck will come.

You must not eat lotus roots on New Year's Day. They will bring you bad luck.

PREDICTING THE WEATHER FOR THE NEW YEAR

A windstorm on New Year's Day means floods later in the year.

The first 12 days in January foretell the weather for the 12 months to come. Good days, good corresponding months. Bad or wet days, wet months (for example, 6th day = 6th month.) The Tennessee Folklore Society Bulletin, XXIV recommends that you write this information on your calendar. Please use the Gregorian one.

A dark New Year is a sign of a good fruit year.

The way the wind blows on January 1 tells you that it will not come out of that direction for more than forty-eight hours or again for forty days.

RITUALS OF LOVE

Want to find a perfect mate? On New Year's Eve, according to the 1986 Old Farmer's Almanac, walk from one room to another while throwing a shoe over your shoulder, then look in the mirror and your future mate's face will appear. (See St.Valentine's Day for more love potions and magic.)

If you want to find out how many months you will have to wait until you marry, Douglas Hill's *Magic and Superstition* suggests this: When the first new moon of the New Year appears, look at the reflections in the bucket of water through a silk handkerchief. The number of moons you see will equal the number of years you must wait.

Girls must not go out early in the morning of New Year's Day because the first unmarried man they meet will be their future husband.

On New Year's night, if you live in the Allegheny mountains, place a gold band in a glass of water, go into a dark cellar, and see your future husband's picture in the bottom of the glass.

If you marry on this day, your mate will be good and true.

If a girl wishes to know whether her future husband will be a stranger or from the vicinity, she can find out by going alone at night on New Year's Eve, standing silently by a peach-tree and shaking its branches. Should a dog bark, her suitor comes from afar, but if a cock crows his home is near.

The New Year's Day celebration, with its long history of merrymaking, partying and gala license, should be a day to reflect and plan for a prosperous and happy future. However, it also bears the ominous New Year's resolutions.

CHAPTER I

NEW YEAR'S DAY - PART II

HOW TO MAKE YOUR RESOLUTIONS WORK

THE RITUAL OF NEW YEAR'S RESOLUTIONS

As the turkey carcass and the bits of tinsel from the dried out tree become only memories, thoughts turn from the dim old year's successes and failures to the bright new year's promise of opportunity and hope. Commitments are made, to self and others ... resolved that this year ... "I will not overeat; I won't procrastinate anymore; I will stop being so negative and fearful; I will quit eating candy bars at night ... and on and on and on ... this year ... I resolve to do, be and have the very best!"

And then, as in some "B" movies of the thirties, the pages are torn from the calendar, and January becomes July becomes November and we are back on the same old horse on the same old carousel with guilt, anger and frustration, resolving, "NEXT YEAR will be...!"

We wonder why New Year's Resolutions don't work! Our heart is certainly in the right place, however often our habits, lifestyles and fears keep us locked into the same old patterns.

When waking up for the first time in the New Year, many feel tired, fat and aimless. Some suggest that that is what prompts New Year's resolutions in the first place, but that is not true. For thousands of years, many religions have recognized that the start of a new year is an ideal time for people to think about penitence and self-improve-ment. A time to say goodbye to the past and to resolve for a better upcoming year.

By that they did not necessarily mean a new diet and a rigorous Nautilus program. Many people think they have been burned once too often by New Year's, and not from leaping over bonfires, but from broken resolutions. Many feel tired from feeling guilty for breaking the resolutions they made last year and not having accomplished as much as they feel they should have or could have.

Free-lance writer Andrew Feinberg suggests that the edgy feelings may not all be from broken resolutions. "Perhaps," he says, "some of the gloom comes from the fact that New Year's Day, while not a Christian holiday, per se, is none-the-less celebrated as the Feast of the Circumcision, the day Jesus found out how much fun it is to be a Jew." "Maybe," he says, "it is those nasty trace memories that make men feel so jittery on the First."

The Gallup poll has asked people about their New Year's resolutions for years, and as recently as the Forties hardly any respondents mentioned weight loss or "working on my pecs." In the 1930's and 1940's such common themes were found as "I will save more money," "I will make more of an effort to get a job," and "I will refrain from getting caught in foreign propaganda." In the fifties and sixties, it was "to make more of myself." In the nineties we find exercising more and losing weight (16%), and cutting out drugs and smoking (14%).

Even though people are beating a path to eventual frustration, they continue making New Year's resolutions. To be exact, 1.8 resolutions per American, says John Norcross, head of Scranton University's Psychology Department, who's spent six years studying the annual exercise of New Year's resolutions.

His findings are not reassuring. Good intentions barely outlast wilting Christmas trees, with one in four resolvers (25%) breaking their promises within a week, according to a 1992 Gallup poll reported in the WALL STREET JOURNAL.

About half (54%) manage to hang on for about a month. But by June, only about 40% can boast of sticking to their goal.

Dr. Norcross says "people tend to rely only on 'good ol' gumption," which is a recipe for failure."

I suspect that those people who were reporting to the pollsters were withholding the truth. From my observations after 21 years in the mental health field, the percentage of broken resolutions is much greater. I think this figure is closer to 99.5% of us who have broken all of our New Year's resolutions, and 95.0% have broken them by the end of January. About one third are resolving to gain or maintain a better relationship, not the 3% reported to the surveyors.

We know that, historically, resolutions don't work and, as Dr. Norcross says, "Excessive reliance on willpower backfires. It's a great American myth."

Even the toasts we use at New Year's tell us that resolutions do not work, such as "May all your troubles during the coming year be as short-lived as your New Years resolutions."

We all know what the definition of a New Year's resolution is: "It's that thing that goes in one year and out the other."

But what is a resolution actually? Well, a resolution, or a commitment, is something that lets us know that most of our weaknesses are really too strong for us.

Why? Why are New Year's resolutions such notorious failures? What are the reasons we have a difficult time making commitments and resolutions work measurably and predictably?

In the first place, ninety-nine percent of the people make New Year's resolutions for the wrong reasons. They do it because everyone else is talking about them and they feel they should make them; or, they do not make them for themselves, but for someone else. Both of those reasons do not work and are doomed for failure.

In the second place, we don't know how to set them up. No one ever really taught us how to set up or make a resolution or commitment. They just said, "Well, just do them." It is almost like our parents when they told us to "Grow up." They never taught us how! One morning we got up and said, "Now I am an adult!" And we still do not know how to be one.

Webster's *Ninth New Collegiate Dictionary* says a resolution, or commitment (they are the exactly the same and are interchangeable) "is a way to engage ourselves physiologically... To move ourselves into action." And without that commitment, without that resolve, we are not going to get those feelings that will engage us and take us into our desired and appropriate action.

When one makes a resolve or a commitment, that act really creates a magical doorway that leads to a pathway of happy and joyful stepping stones to wellness and success.

It is an engagement. And that is very important. It is an engagement of physical feelings. It is not wishful thinking, it is not just positive thinking, because we have all noticed that many times we will think positively, and we will set up good goals, and nothing happens. Why? What did not happen? We did not get the feelings that give us the behavior that we want.

Keeping resolutions is a lot like curing your phobias. There's a certain way to do it. . . steps that have to be followed in order to succeed with resolutions or goals.

PHOBIAS AND NEW YEAR'S RESOLUTIONS

Fear is the third and major reason why people either do not make resolutions or commitments, or fail to keep them once made.

Fear is the biggest blocker and, at the Phobia Institute and Stress Management Centers, we have isolated various fears associated with the New Year. I am sure you can think of others.

Tropophobia - the biggest fear of all - is the fear of change. And we hate to change. Why? Because when making a commitment (or a resolve), we create change and that change short circuits our old behavior patterns, our habituated nerve pathways, and we invariably revert back to our old habits unless there is some kind of intervention made. We are creatures of habit.

In my book *Keying: The Power of Positive Feelings*, I devote nearly an entire chapter to the phenomenon called the "comfort zone." Basically, the "comfort zone" is an area of familiarity, not necessarily comfortable, that has been so strongly conditioned in the nerve pathways that the behavior in that area has become a habit. If we get too far out of that comfort zone of familiarity, or go beyond it too quickly or without preparing for it, we begin to feel anxious and stressed.

Using New Year's resolutions to break habits usually does not work because the messages of "resolve," "will power," "burning desire" or "positive thinking" do not get deep enough into the physiology. Physical tension causes a short circuit and prevents the reception of clear signals into the body.

When that happens, we will do anything to get back into our comfort zone. That is why people who win a lot of money often end up wasting it, investing poorly and losing it or even getting physically or emotionally ill. Often you have seen movie stars who quickly escalate into fame and fortune and then self-destruct because of not having prepared for the phenomenon of the "comfort zone." Like an addict, they literally become addicted to unhappiness and mediocrity.

To cure a phobia, you have to change your behavior. You also have to change your behavior if you are going to keep a resolution you have made. Some people fear change so much that they do not make any resolutions at all. So, tropophobia, the fear of change, is the biggest fear we have and it is that fear that usually destroys our chances of success in keeping our resolutions.

Another fear is katagelophobia - the excessive fear and avoidance of being ridiculed, put down and embarrassed in social situations. It falls into the psychiatrist's diagnostic category of Social Phobias and is a big inhibitor to successful goal achievement.

Kakorraphiaphobia is another big anxiety provoking barrier that keeps us from making and keeping resolutions and commitments. Kakorraphiaphobia is the fear of failure. The fear of looking bad, worthless or not capable. This fear of failure is also associated with the three P's of procrastination. Perfectionism leads to Paralysis and that leads to Procrastination. Immobilized and unable to act because of fearing to fail.

All of these fears can be lumped into one big fear, absolutely the biggest, most insidious, most harmful, most agonizing and most predominant fear in the world. And that is giraffeophobia. No, that is not the fear of long necks, long legs or spotted animals from Africa. Giraffeophobia --- the fear of sticking your neck out.

We are all afraid of sticking our necks out, and we are afraid to go to the top. That is one of the most incredible phenomenon. But we are automatically driven to go higher and higher and to do better and better. And when we do get richer, when we do get happier, and when we do get more wonderful relationships - it's like Reverend Peggy Bassett said, "The higher you go up the ladder of success, the more your posterior shows." And that is it. The fear of mooning the world! It is also related to the fear of success or eleutherophobia, and the fear of responsibility which is hypergiaphobia.

There was a federal judge by the name of Judge Medina. He is quoted as saying, "If you go out and do something worthwhile, I guarantee you, you will catch hell for it." That's about it, isn't it?

However, if we really think about it, that's what we really want isn't it? We want the jealousy, we want the envy of our associates, loved ones and our brothers and sisters. We work all our lives to get it. It's another incredible phenomenon. We work very hard to get it, then once we get it, we feel as if we have to throw it away. However, the problem is, we generally do not recognize envy and jealousy as they actually are, admiration and respect. That jealousy, when we are happy, making a lot of money and more spiritual, is really admiration and respect.

So, the next time that someone is jealous of you because you are rich, or you are happy or you are full of bliss and the spirit of God, say to them, "Thank you very much for admiring me. I appreciate that very much!" That's the truth of it isn't it? I have been working all my life trying to out-do my brother, Victor. And when on occasions I do, I feel guilty. These feelings must be overcome in order to get our resolutions to work.

OTHER REASONS NEW YEAR'S RESOLUTIONS FAIL

OK. We have all these fears. Plus, we have other reasons why resolutions do not work, including focusing on what could go wrong, trying too hard, thinking they are too heavy and no fun and setting them up too vaguely and not very specifically. Some goals are too self-serving and too short-sighted. We lack control over the mind, feeling and actions to keep us on track.

There are all kinds of reasons why they fail. However, before we go any further, let us realize that there are only two kinds of people. Then, let us examine the differences between goals, commitments and purposes. And finally, we will look at specific ways, or steps, with which to overcome the blocks and barriers that people use as reasons for not reaching their goals.

I have found that there are two kinds of people. The first kind are the ones who can make commitments and get things done. They commit to things bigger than they are. They are overtly spiritual and happy. They are rich in more ways than one; they have wonderful, loving relationships. They are out there in the community participating in life. And they're just "doing it."

The second type of people, on the other hand, are the ones who have all of the reasons why they are not doing anything worthwhile, the reasons why they are not happy or rich, or the reasons why they do not have good relationships.

GOALS, COMMITMENTS AND PURPOSES

Let us look at those people who just "do it" with no excuses. They just let go of the reasons, they abandon the pickiyunish resentments and the petty blames, and all that. The fact is that if you find yourself blaming something or someone for not succeeding, or have petty jealousies, then those are your signposts to let you know you are not committed in some area.

In fact, any area in which you find yourself miserable is the exact area in which you have no goals or commitments.

We are not talking only about goals. There is a difference between goals and commitments. A goal has a target. That's something you can reach. A **goal** is **fixed in time and space. It has a beginning and an end**.

A **commitment** is made **out of time and out of space. It has no beginning or end**. It is **fixed out of time and space.** That's why I say that a commitment is a **spiritual connection with God,** a spiritual connection with Universal Law. A commitment is **on-going.** It is like an **aim** towards something. It is a **direction.**

It is like shooting a bow and arrow. If you shoot an arrow hard enough, the arrow will just go around the earth on and on and on. The aim will be the same. It is not until you put a target in front of the arrow that it hits the target and stops. However, the aim is still there. It remains. That is the same thing as with a commitment. It continues. It is an energy force. A commitment (or resolve) puts movement into a goal. It is the trigger that puts a goal into action. It is an act. You act because you make the commitment. And that gives the energy and the movement and the power, as well as the aim, to reach the target.

But we also need purpose. A goal does not do any good, and neither does a commitment, without purpose. They are worthless. We have to have all three.

A **purpose** is the **reason for doing something**. Purpose is the **path**. Without purpose, all else is worthless. We need a path on which to travel. And, we have to make a purpose that is bigger than ourselves. The purpose of serving others in which we glorify God, is the biggest of all, by the way.

Actually, we would have all that we need if we had only the purpose of glorifying God. Jesus, Buddha, Rabbi Hillel, Sri Ramakrishna, Yogananda, Holmes and Troward, all of the great religious leaders of the world said the same thing, "We are all here for one reason. We are here for only one purpose and that is to glorify God." That is not a superstition either, it is the truth.

To glorify God means to prove the Law of Universal Order. It is the law of Cause and Effect. That is, what goes around, comes around, or what you sow is what you will reap. God is begging us to prove the Law that serving others will give us everything we want. And that purpose will give us the reason to get up in the morning. We don't usually get up easily unless we really are willing and able to help other human beings.

Most of us know of Zig Ziglar, the famous motivational speaker. He said what epitomizes this truth for me. He said, "Go find out what people need. And once you find out what people need, then figure out how to give it to them, how to get it to them. Then, you are going to be successful, happy, blissful and rich."

He even went further than that with rich. He said, "If you commit yourself to serving other people, dollar bills will come around your back yard to find out what kind of person you are." Isn't that great? I just love it. And it is the bottom-line truth.

That is a humbling thing, though. It means that we have to let go, with abandon, our vain ideas of separateness. It really is a vain idea of ours that we are separated from the oneness of God when, in reality, a great sage said, "we are only an idea on the wings of God." We are more than that, we are one with God. We are the wave, and God is the ocean. But, we can only know that when we have committed ourselves to glorify God. When we commit ourselves to do that, everything else will begin to fall into place.

What we have then is a goal which is the target, a commitment that generates the actions and the purpose which is the path. Now we have it all. Now we can more easily glorify God and get what we want. If the term "God" is troublesome for you, use a term with which you are comfortable like Nature or the unconscious mind. It does not matter. The truth of it will not change; when our intent is clear and our outcome is to serve others, we will be predictably successful.

Now let us take a look at some of the stepping stones with which we can make our goals, purposes and commitments more predictable and more measurable.

STEPPING STONES TO MAKING
RESOLUTIONS WORK

When studying linguistics, I learned that most people make negative resolutions by saying things like "I'm not going to overeat," "I won't procrastinate anymore" and "I will stop wasting money on the lottery," which don't work. The reason they are ineffective is that, linguistically, what follows the negative in our thinking, or in our resolving, will be obeyed exactly as if it were a deep hypnotic command, and will be obeyed at an unconscious, conscious and behavioral level. It sets us up to respond exactly in the opposite way. If you resolve "I won't do this," you will.

Think of the time when your child was walking across the living room with some hot chocolate in his hand and you said, "Don't spill the chocolate!" And swooooosh, he spilled the chocolate. What follows the negative will always be obeyed at some level. In my cassette program "Through The Briar Patch," I have people reach down and touch their knee and as they do, I say, "Don't think pink elephant." Try it. Touch your knee and don't think "pink elephant." You will have a pink elephant on your knee for a long time, but that is OK, it is a harmless pink elephant.

Instead of using negatives, or "stops," make your resolutions or goals in positive, specific terms: "I will be fit and trim and weigh 175 pounds," or "I will have an active life and have healthy lungs." In other words focus on beneficial and precise outcomes.

FOCUS ON THE OUTCOME
RATHER THAN THE PROBLEM

There is a universal motivation formula that is important to know. The formula is "What you think about, you begin to feel; what you feel, you begin to do; what you do, you have or tend to become." It is the think/feel/do/have motivational law.

Notice that *feelings* precede behavior, not thinking! That's why positive thinking, psychotherapy or holding a positive mental attitude do not work a lot of times and are not predictable. It is because, generally, they are not strong enough. They are not developed in a way to give us the needed physical feelings that will give us the desired action or movement.

Look at what happens when you focus on your problem. You think of, and you *feel,* the problem. Have you noticed how much depressed and gloomy people talk about depression and gloom? Have you noticed that poor people talk about poverty, sick people talk about sickness? Why? Because that is what they feel and what we feel we also talk about. We get caught in what I call the think-feel, feel-think "fear loop" and we can not or do not know how to get out of it.

However, when we focus on the outcome, when we focus on the solution, when we focus on what we want, we engage our conscious and unconscious mind, which connect with the superconscious mind. That gives us the trajectory which begins to guide us effortlessly to our desired happiness and success.

Notice, I say "effortlessly." As I said on the Oprah Winfrey Show, "Don't try too hard. Why? Because a push gets a push. It backs up on itself." It is like trying to walk up a shale mountain too fast or too hard. You take two or three steps up and you slide down one or two. You hurriedly take another two or three steps and, again, you slide down one or two.

What we need to do is to relax... and be here now... and just slowly and effortlessly walk up the shale mountain with commitment and purpose and faith ... and we will go right to the top of the mountain, right to the apex. Then we can, with panoramic vision, look over the entire beautiful valley and into the choices, the multitude of choices, that God gives us every day in this bountiful world.

Research has shown that we have to keep effortlessly focused with an eye on the outcome and the goals for our commitments to more predictably come true.

BE SPECIFIC - STAY AWAY FROM GENERALIZATIONS

Did you ever notice, when you think of your fears, worries or depressions, how big and looming your mental pictures are, and how clear and specific they are? Have you ever noticed how clear, specific and loud your negative self talk is when you are thinking of something that makes you feel bad? And, conversely, how vague the thoughts of happiness, wealth and abundance are? That's a hint to making your resolutions more predictable.

The more specific your ideas are, the more specific your goals are, and the more easily you're going to attain them. Because, again, your unconscious mind launches you on that trajectory and you begin to see what I call the "deli sign phenomenon." Have you ever noticed that when you are hungry, and you are driving down the boulevard, you see more deli signs, restaurant signs and more cafe signs than you do at any other time? That is an automatic, unconscious operation of the mind. It is important to notice that the deli signs were already there. Let me repeat, already there. The mind body "set," the thinking and feelings, allows us to see what was already there.

Some call it the law of cause and effect. Others called it the law of self-fulfilling prophecy, the law of mental equivalence or the law of circulation. I call it the "deli sign phenomenon." It is an automatic operation of the mind ---actually it's a universal law.

When we are focused with more specificity on our goals, more intense feelings are created (specific thought = more intense feelings, vague thoughts = vague feelings). And that sets up the trajectory so we can begin to see "deli signs" of abundance, love, happiness and spirituality. Or any other desired "deli sign."

Another way to make these commitments work and to make life more fun and more effortless is to ....

FOCUS YOUR EYES BEYOND THE GOAL

Now that we have our goals clearly defined, we must focus beyond them. As I say in my audio cassette programs, once you learn how to "key in" all the feelings of happiness, health and spirituality you want, what are you going to do? Once you achieve your goals, then what is your life going to be like? Now that you have everything you want, how is your life going to be different?

That is the same thing we need to do in order to make resolutions work. Go beyond the goal. We must learn from Carl Lewis, the famous Olympic runner. When the starting gun is about to go off, he sees himself all the way back home, talking to his friends and relatives about having won the race he is about to run.

So, we must focus beyond our goal. That will make our goal, which appeared big at one time, now simply a small stepping stone. It does not appear as a block or barrier any more. It depends on our point of view. It is just a step to get us to the next thing we are after. And it becomes very easy.

When you are looking beyond your goals and you have reduced your goals to simple stepping stones to get there, then you merely have to take only one step at a time. You get up in the morning one day at a time and you take only one step at a time. Everything becomes a lot easier and you will be joyful and happy. In fact, happiness, by its very definition, is overcoming "blocks" and "barriers" while going toward our goals. Happiness is not achieving the outcome, it is going after it. That is why it is so important to de-brief, or de-program, after attaining a goal.

DE-BRIEFING

When you have achieved a particular goal, stop the programming. "De-program" it. The process of ending or de-programming goals is just as important as the process of formulating new ones.

Astronauts de-brief every time they land after orbiting the earth. The process is not just to gather information, but it is also used to get them out of orbit. We automatically use de-briefing when, after returning from a hectic day at the office or driving on a crowded expressway, we tell our story. We get home and tell our mate, or our friends, what a terrible traffic jam we encountered, or what a busy day we had at work. That is unconscious de-briefing. To end the programming on achieved or thwarted goals, we should purposely de-brief.

Larry's goal was to get married. He was a successful psychotherapist and he got married. Then he got divorced. He got married again. Then he got divorced, and got married again. Larry never "noticed" that he had completed his goal and so he kept on "accomplishing" it. Larry kept on getting married!

Chuck's goal was to make a million dollars. He was a brilliant motion picture producer, and he made a million dollars. Then he lost it, actually frittered it away. Then he made another million. Then he lost it. . . and so on. Like Larry, Chuck did not stop to "notice" that he'd reached his goal.

Once you see that you have reached your goal, stop the programming. That disc is ready for storage. De-brief. Talk to your mate or a friend or yourself... just like the astronauts do when they return to earth.

Write it down. "This is what I wanted. This is what I saw, heard, felt, thought and did when I was accomplishing my goal." This technique is also good when you change your goals or did not get what you wanted.

Continue de-briefing until you begin to get a sense of "So what? What's next?" This is an automatic experience. And when you reach this, you're ready to start setting up a new goal, or goals, in that area.

TAKE A RISK AND BREAK THE RULES

After we have focused beyond our goals, we must allow ourselves the privilege and thrill of risk taking. Give up the fears of making a mistake. Every decision will always be made with insufficient data.

To be more successful in fulfilling our commitments, we want to start learning how to take chances, and learning how to break the rules. Rules are what we generally know as facts. We do not want to deal with facts. The facts are 95% of the people on this planet are miserable, 95% of the people over age 65 are not financially independent, 95% of the people do not know how to make commitments work. These facts are usually interpreted as rules. We want to break the rules. We want to go beyond apparent facts into the truth.

There was a physician in the mid 1800's by the name of Ignaz Semilwies who was booted out of the medical profession because he had the audacity to suggest to his fellow doctors that they wash their hands before they examine their female patients in preparation for childbirth. Can you imagine? He was ostracized and actually died in an insane asylum. And today he is heralded as the father of antiseptics. Can you imagine that somebody's heresy, at that time, is now today's truth?

He broke the rules. He ignored the facts. And that is what we have to do. I say in my seminars, "Shoot for the moon! Shoot for the moon! The worst thing that could happen if you miss is that you'll end up with the stars." And that is not all that bad, is it?

Zig Ziglar says, "You have to go out on a limb...because that's where the fruit is." So shoot for the moon and go beyond the facts into the truth.

CONTROLLING YOUR MIND AND YOUR FEELINGS

Once you have set up your goals correctly, being able to control your mind and your bodily feelings is a must. Remember, what you think about you do, and what you do determines what you have. You have to get the desired feelings in order to get the movement you want. Many times, focusing on the outcome and holding it with specificity isn't good enough. When that happens, use Keying and Refocusing techniques to guarantee your success.

What is Keying? Keying is a predictable and measurable way to lock in any feelings you want regardless of what you are thinking or what's going on around you. With Keying you can lock in, and unlock, any feelings you want, wherever you want, and you can be motivated whenever and wherever you want.

The Refocusing technique, on the other hand, is an easy method of controlling the mind in order to control your feelings. (Both Keying and Refocusing will be covered in depth in Chapter IX, Part II, on Christmas and the holiday blues.)

So, Keying and Refocusing are tools that are considered major contributions in the world of motivational sciences. They are quantum leaps, the link between religion and behavioral science. They are the reason I have been demonstrating their power throughout the world.

When you can control your commitments you have confidence, you have faith. And what are commitments and faith? They are feelings. They are not simply ideas. Confidence and faith for a commitment are feelings and it is feelings that motivate and move us.

Using Keying and Refocusing is breaking the rules. This is taking a risk because you are going to notice fast, yet safe change. You will begin to notice quick ways to wash away phobias and stress.

You will begin using predictable ways in which to have abundance, happiness and joy that are fast and painless.

They will give you the feelings that will initiate the behavior and action that will connect your conscious mind, your unconscious mind (which is the body memories), and the superconscious mind. Then you do not have to do anything - except get out of the way and look for the "deli signs."

HAVE FUN

Above all, you must have some fun. If you are not enjoying yourself doing what you are doing, then you are not doing the right thing or you are not doing it right. You have to have a fun, playful frame of mind in order for your resolutions to complete themselves. All the Masters teach us to rejoice in the loving play of God. Bliss and happiness can be ours.

If you have trouble doing this, then act "as if" you are doing it and your unconscious mind will do the rest. You can't think yourself to happy actions, but you can act your way to happy thinking.

Another reason why most New Year's resolutions are quickly broken —- 50% last no longer than two weeks — is that we try to do it only once a year. We should not pick just one day of the year, but we should implement them throughout the year. We should learn to make every day the beginning of a new year. We should celebrate with wonder and curiosity every day as a fresh beginning. I teach my patients how to start each day, just like a child, by saying, "I wonder, I wonder what wonderful thing is going to happen today. I wonder." Then it will be fun all the time.

SUMMARY AND APHORISMS

Learn to face your "limitations" and do something anyway.

Be sure your intent is clear and real, and that your outcome will serve others.

Be specific. Stay away from generalizations.

Stay away from negatives such as "don'ts" and "stops."

Learn to focus on the outcome you want instead of the problems.

Focus beyond your goals. This makes the goal only a stepping stone.

Keep your goals simple...avoid overloading yourself.

Take a risk, break the rules, ignore the "facts" and play with abandon. When you do, you will operate on the edge of control, the edge of your reflexes, and God will smile on you.

Learn to use the Keying process and Refocusing techniques to help you hold the "as if" feelings.

Practice having a sense of gratitude and thankfulness. This will combat the myth of self-suffering and ward off the negative, cynical view of the "scardy cat."

Make your resolutions fun. Your resolutions are not going to be successful if you are not having fun fulfilling your goals and life does not fill you with wonder.

Let us remember the old Irish toast "As we start the New Year, Let's get down on our knees to thank God we're on our feet."

JUST TO CLINCH IT FOR YOU, REMEMBER TO HAVE PLENTY OF CINDRA'S HOPPIN' JOHN SOUP.

CHAPTER II

SAINT VALENTINE'S DAY -

LOVE, ROMANCE AND COURTSHIP

HAVE YOU EVER WONDERED...

... why Feb. 14th was specifically chosen to be the holiday of love, romance and courtship?

... if it really was named after a martyr called Valentine, or if he even existed?

... how love birds became connected to St. Valentine's Day and, specifically, why the dove?

... how Cupid with his arrows piercing the heart, heart symbols and red roses become associated with St. Valentine's Day?

... why we call the person we love "sweetheart" or "honey?"

... where sayings like "vinegar valentines" or "he leaves a bitter taste in my mouth" came from?

... where the metaphor "carrying our hearts on our sleeves" originated?

... if "Love Apples" are really apples?

... where the saying, "she's a hot tomato" originated?

... why chocolate is one of the world's favorite love tokens?

...why we often say "I'm crazy about you" or "I'm nuts over you?"

... why, with all these good feelings around, so many people are depressed, lonely, and suicidal around this time of year?

... how St. Valentine's Day fears are different from the typical phobias?

... if people can actually become addicted to loneliness, fear and unhappiness?

... if these people need or should seek psychiatric or psychological help?

... what are some folklore "cures" and love potion recipes are that have been used to attract and keep a sweetheart?

... how to win a sweetheart using suggestions from psychologists?

... what up-to-date technique can help couples maintain an ongoing relationship or make it even more joyful?

... if "honesty" really is the best policy?

... if hiding the dried tongue of a turtle dove in a girl's room really causes her to love you forever?

With one holiday fading, another comes: St. Valentines Day. On February 14th our hearts turn lightheartedly to love, and especially to expressing affection to that someone special. Cupid, with his bow and arrows, will been seen on cards everywhere. Hearts pierced with golden arrows, turtle doves, red roses --- all the symbols have to do with love and courtship. Where each symbol came from and how they were all laced together, like a Valentine's Day card, forms an intriguing history and a lovely story of the origin of St. Valentine's Day. Some of the stories have beginnings so ancient they are dim with time.

ORIGINS

The actual origin is so ancient that it has left scholars unsure, but there is no question of its importance. Jane M. Hatch in *The American Book of Days* suggests that the association of St. Valentine and lovers grew out of the similarity between *Valentine* and the Norman word *galantin*, the name of a saint which means "a lover of women." They say that Galantin's Day (the *g* is often pronounced *v*) added to the confusion.

Records show, however, another theory of the association with lovers. This speculation says that more than a century before Christ, on the eve and day of February 15, an ancient Roman festival, *Lupercalia,* was observed to ensure fertility and health. It was a ritual celebration of courtship, mating and good crops.

Edna Barth, in her lovely and most delightful book, *Hearts, Cupids, and Red Roses: The Story of the Valentine Symbols*, tells of a romance and courtship practice where, on the evening of *Lupercalia,* February 14th, Roman youths would draw names of girls from an urn. The name drawn was to be their partner during the festival. (When I was in elementary school, an echo of this practice was observed, except that we used a big box decorated with red hearts and cupids instead of an urn.)

According to legend, the festival was to honor *Faunus,* who, like the Greek *Pan,* was the god of the crops. Two youths, the story goes, were blessed by their priests and ran through the Roman streets swinging about them goatskin thongs called *Februa.* The Latin word, *Februatio,* the act of lashing with the sacred thongs, was for the purpose of "purification." From it comes our name for February. It was believed that if a young woman was touched by the thongs she would be better able to bear children.

The Roman solders, in the first century before Christ, took with them the customs of Lupercalia, and that is where we got our customs of drawing names for partners or sweethearts on February 14th.

By the fourth century, the Church had become the legal religion of the Empire. The church fathers, as hard as they tried, were unable to abolish the "pagan" festival, the derogatory name they gave to the older religions. So, in a true resolute spirit, "when you can't beat 'em, join 'em," the Church assigned it a Christian name, "St. Valentine's Day."

The celebration of St. Valentine's Day was banned more than once and in more than one country. However, do what it might, the church could not erase the meaning and memories of the ancient celebration of mating. The memories lived on in the minds of the populace. In 1660 the good Charles II restored the day. Eventually the courting practices were revived and men once again began to send love tokens and proposals on February 14th.

Because of Great Britain, the advent of the printing of greeting cards, the strong need of the human spirit for love and the continued infatuation of children for the holiday, Saint Valentine's Day is now observed more than ever.

WHO WAS SAINT VALENTINE?

Who was St. Valentine or did he ever really exist? Again, scholars seem to differ. Early church records list a number of martyrs by this name and feasts were held on February 14th for each of them. It is possible, however, that none of them had anything to do with the festival of love, mating and courtship.

There are many legends about these various Valentines. One legend tells of a time when, in the third century after Christ, Claudius II needed more soldiers to fight his wars. He believed that love and marriage made men want to stay home and not go to war.(A pretty good idea). Anyway, he decreed that no one was to marry or become engaged. A priest named Valentine defied Claudius by performing marriage ceremonies, was imprisoned for it and put to death.

A favorite of mine is the legend that tells of a Valentine who was thrown in jail because he helped persecuted Christians. While in prison he restored the sight of the jailor's blind daughter, Julia. When he was put to death, he sent a farewell letter to the girl and signed it "From your Valentine." Whether or not it is true, it is a lovely story.

LOVEBIRDS AND DOVES

In the Middle Ages, it was believed that birds mated on St. Valentine's Day. The missel thrush, the partridge, and the blackbird really did mate in the middle of February. Seeing that, people thought all birds did and, according to some, that is probably why we attached the date of the 14th to love, courtship and mating.

As love birds became connected with St. Valentine's Day, the dove emerged as the most favorite of symbols on valentines, bearing a message alone or in pairs. Why, specifically, the dove? In mythology, it was sacred to Venus and other love deities. Barth said that "from the time of Noah, doves had served as sacred messengers." The Bible speaks of doves as messengers, and they are spoken of in the Song of Solomon as... "the time of singing of birds is come, and the voice of the turtle is heard in our land." (turtle is short for turtle dove.)

Also, doves mate for life; are seen sharing the duties of caring for their babies; loving and cooing; and have long been symbols of romantic love. In many lands, ancient and modern, doves have been seen as magical and have been used to divine the future.

CUPID AND HIS HEART PIERCING ARROWS

The ancient, mythological Roman god, *Cupid,* the symbol of passionate and playful love, is the son of Venus, the goddess of love and beauty. The Greek's counterpart of Cupid is Eros, son of Aphrodite. We can see that we have the Greeks to thank for our terms *erotica* and *aphrodisiac.*

One myth tells the story of a time when Cupid fell deeply in love with the beautiful Psyche, a mere mortal. Venus, Cupid's mother, grew jealous and tricked Psyche into doing a series of tasks of ever increasing difficulty. When Psyche peeked into the "box of beauty," she was struck into a deep slumber.

Cupid eventually came along and found her. With his love, he removed the sleep and put it back into the box. And, with one of his arrows, he touched her heart and she awoke. Moved by her undying love for Cupid, the gods made her a god and they lived happily ever after.

It is interesting to see how Cupid's appearance changed over the centuries. In ancient times, he was the symbol of love; a young, handsome, Adonis-like mythological man. Now, he is a chubby little playful cherub.

MY HEART PINES FOR YOU

Hearts, according to scholars, were believed by our ancient ancestors to contain the soul. The Egyptians thought it to be the center of intelligence and reasoning. Even today, the way in which we talk of "heartsick" feelings or sending "heartfelt" greetings sounds as if we believe our hearts contain our emotions. Lovesickness and heartaches occur when our hearts have been pierced with Cupid's arrows. We lose all sense of reason, and all of our intellectual faculties, which proves that the Egyptians may have been on the right track and knew what they were talking about!

There was a quaint Medieval custom in England, and other countries of Europe, of drawing names for a partner. Barth said that in many areas, the young men would pin the names of their partners on their sleeves for a week. This is where the idea of "carrying our hearts on our sleeves" originated. Nowadays, it is a way in which to describe those who are quick to show their feelings and we speak of them as "wearing their hearts on their sleeves."

ROSES ARE RED

Flowers were associated with love tokens long before there was any Valentine's Day. Their beauty and scented fragrance was always tied to love and romance.

Red roses were sacred to *Bacchus*, the god of wine and joy, and Venus, the goddess of love and beauty, and also were connected to Cupid. Barth indicated that from the time of Solomon, the primary flower linked to love and romance has been the rose. It served as a love token long before valentines ever existed. Cleopatra of Egypt covered the floor with roses before receiving her lover, Mark Anthony.

One mythological origin of the rose, she related, is told in a story about Cupid. He was carrying a vase of sweet nectar to the gods on Mount Olympus and spilled it on ground. On that spot roses grew.

Another myth tells of the reason roses have thorns on them. The soft west wind, *Zephyr*, one day opened a lovely rose and Cupid bent over to kiss the elegant petals. When he did, he was stung by an irate bee hiding inside. Venus got so angry that she had Cupid shoot some bees and string them up on one of his arrows. Then she planted the string of dead bee stings on the rose stems. The stings became thorns, and from that day on roses have had thorns.

It was believed by ancient Romans that anything discussed under a rose was *sub rosa*, and was to be kept a secret. We still use this Latin expression today to describe something that is to be kept confidential.

ST. VALENTINE'S DAY GOES TO AMERICA

Saint Valentine's Day came to the United States with the Puritans in 1629, but the practices went against the grain of the church fathers. Besides, they had many other more serious things to attend to. Around one hundred years passed before the memories and longings for the day of romance and courtship could no longer be kept down. That is when the first valentine cards began to appear.

These stories are only the tip of the iceberg in the history of the symbols associated with the day of courtship. They each have fascinating stories of their own. I highly recommend Edna Barth's thoroughly delightful book, and *The American Book of Days,* for many more.

ST. VALENTINE'S DAY CAN BE A DARK DAY

Yes, St. Valentine's Day is the day when most of us express our love to that someone special, that "sweetheart." However, that is not true for far too many. This day of "love in bloom" can bring out feelings more akin to those of poet Dorothy Parker, "...And love is a thing that can never go wrong...and I am the Queen of Romania!"

With the divorce rate over 50%, for those who have lost their mates because of death or separation or those singles who do not have a "special one," St. Valentine's Day can be a very painful day of darkness.

Like the reported tormented ghosts of the Chicago St. Valentine's Day Massacre in 1939 where seven fell dead, millions have an agonizing sense of loneliness which brings on depression, physical illness and an increase in the incidents of suicide around this day. These afflictions often become phobias, such as *Amoraphobia*, the fear of love, *Katagelophobia,* the fear of failure and *Tropophobia,* the fear of change, as well as other fears.

The following phobias are associated with St. Valentine's Day:

Birds and the Bees	Orintho/Api-phobia
Blushing	Ereuthophobia
Commitment	Committereophobia - Obligaphobia
Flowers	Anlophobia
Furs	Dorapophobia
People	Anthropophobia
Jealousy	Zelophobia
Love	Amoraphobia
Marriage	Gamophobia

(I thought Johnny Carson had that phobia, but he proved me wrong.)

Men	Androphobia
Novelty	Cainophobia or Neophobia
Physical love	Arotophobia
Pleasure	Hedonophobia

Disease	Nosophobia
Pregnancy	Matensiophobia
Sex	Genophobia
Sexual Intercourse	Coitophobia or Cypridophobia
Strangers	Xenophobia
Touching or being touched	Haphephobia
Uncovering the body	Gymnophobia
Women	Gynophobia
Young girls	Pathenophobia

The symptoms can range from mild anxiety to extremely severe panic attacks.

These fears are different from the typical phobias only in degree. All negative feelings are fear based and when we fear something, it is because we have lost control of our minds (not lost our minds), and lost control of our physical feelings. The pictures in our minds are bigger than life and very clear. The internal self-talk is resounding extremely loud in our minds. These are what cause the fearful, isolated and depressing feelings.

People can actually become addicted to loneliness, fear and unhappiness; addicted in the sense that, as any addict, they have an unwanted habit over which they have lost control. (See the section about the "comfort zone" in Chapter I on New Year's Day) They don't want to feel bad, by the way. That is a theory still held onto by the old outdated, obsolete psychologies. They are not mentally ill. They have lost control and need some kind of intervention to regain it.

Generally, these people do not need and should not seek traditional psychiatric or psychological help. Research reported in *The Myth of Neurosis* by Garth Wood, the *Brain/Mind Bulletin* and others, has shown that psychotherapy at best is no better than a placebo, a sugar pill, and at worst could be detrimental, even hazardous, to ones physical, mental or emotional health.

James Hillman, in his book, *We've Had a Hundred Years of Psychotherapy and The World's Getting Worse,* goes even further. He contends that psychotherapy is actually causing the world's economic and social deterioration and breakdown.

With the advent of the AIDS epidemic, certain cautions are definitely needed when establishing a new relationship. However, the widespread fear of AIDS, and its appropriateness, has put only a bit of a damper on St. Valentine's Day. As long as one is discreet and morally discriminating, a good time is still to be had. In this case, I suggest that some paranoia may be fitting.

See the chapters on New Year's Day and Christmas holiday blues for more information on how to regain control of our feelings, our minds, and our lives safely and predictably.

"SWEETHEART," "HONEY" AND OTHER DELICIOUS THINGS

In a different vein, there has not been one radio or television talk show host who has not been intrigued as to why we call the person with whom we are in love "sweetheart," or "honey."

Researchers have found that when we are "in love," a chemical is produced in the body called *phenylethylamine* or *phenylalanine.* This drug is responsible for the erratic, psychotic behavior we exhibit when Cupid hits his mark. Phenylalanine is chemically related to the family of amphetamines.

We can stay up all night and work all the next day when in love, and there is no such thing as "geographically undesirable!" Androstenol, a pheromone or chemical sex attractant which heightens our interest, is also released. All these self-induced drugs create a very sweet taste in our mouths. When we utter the words "luscious," "sweetheart," "delicious," "sugar pie," or "honey," linguistically, we are actually expressing our real experience, the sweetness we taste in our mouths.

On the other hand, when we feel disgusted, disturbed or depressed, we say, "It's a bitter world out there," "He leaves a sour taste in my mouth," "She's a bitter pill to swallow," or "That smells fishy to me." All of the expressions, and there are many more I am sure you can think of, are verbalizations of our experiences. Poets knew this centuries before the linguists.

And that is where the term "vinegar valentines" comes from. They were spiteful, "comical" or sarcastic valentines usually sent by mail.

LOVE APPLES ARE NOT APPLES, YOU SAY?

During the Civil War and the Gay Nineties, tomatoes were thought to be unfit to eat. They were found only in the garden, were considered love tokens and were called *love apples*. Aztecs also considered tomatoes poison and used them for decorations and divination.

Apples, historically, have been tokens of love and fertility. The Norse gods ate apples to stay young and scholars say that the Hebrew women drank and washed with the sap of an apple for fertility. They have also been used for divining and fortune telling since ancient times. However,leave it to the Spaniards. They brought the tomato seeds to us from South America and believed the nightshade vegetable to be an aphrodisiac.

So, "love apples" are not really apples, they are tomatoes and historically are an emblem of passion and love. That, by the way, is the origination of the derogatory saying, "She's really a hot tomato!"

CHOCOLATE - THE WORLD'S FAVORITE LOVE TOKEN

Why is chocolate one of the world's most favorite love tokens? It is, curious enough, rich in phenylethylamine or phenylalanine, the chemical that is related to the amphetamines and is responsible for our erratic behavior when we are in love. Remember that sweet taste in our mouths? Well, being drugged by our own chemicals is also the reason we often say things like, "I'm 'crazy' about you," "I'm nuts over you," and "Baby, you're driving me out of my mind!"

WANT SOME POTIONS TO ATTRACT LOVE?

Swallow the heart of a white dove, point downward, while resting your hand on your lover's shoulder. This will ensure his or her loving you forever.

Put a pinch of powdered wild gander's foot in your lover's coffee, tea or milk. The wild gander is always faithful and so will your lover be after drinking it.

If you think that's bad, consider the Australian aborigines who prepare a love potion from the testicles of kangaroos!

Walk around the block with your mouth full of water; if you don't swallow it, you will marry within the year.

Offer your lover a double-fudge sundae to start the love chemicals flowing, then give her or him a great big hug.

Cry a lot, exercise briskly and drink large amounts of fluid, but stay away from pigs. According the 1986 *Old Farmer's Almanac*, androstenol, a chemical substance found in tears, sweat and urine, is thought to be a pheromone, a sex attractant. In one experiment, subjects wearing masks were more attracted to people injected with the chemical, androstenol, than those who were not. Results are being questioned and attempts to replicate the study are being conducted. However, androstenol has been proven successful in inducing female pigs to assume the mating stance.

Give your prospective mate beer, lemonade, or cider containing a teaspoonful of your own powdered fingernails for faithful love.

Kiss as many people as you possibly can. According to Dr. Bubba Nicholson, whose findings appeared in the *British Journal of Dermatology,* kissing is a way for us to taste and smell semiochemicals on another's skin. Semiochemicals transmit biological signals of compatibility and attraction, says Dr. Nicholson.

Want to tell if your love will be faithful? Cut a lemon in half and rub both pieces on the four corners of your bed. Put the lemon halves under your pillow and go to sleep. If you dream of your love, he or she will be faithful. If you don't, watch out.

Take walks in high, dangerous places. Scientists found that emotional arousal can induce feelings of attraction. In the study, one group of men walked across a swaying footbridge and the other a sturdy concrete structure. An attractive female researcher met them halfway. She asked them some counterfeit questions and slipped each her telephone number. More of the footbridge men called her.

Bring red and white rose petals to a boil in exactly 385 drops of water for the sixteenth part of an hour. Then, add three drops of this potion into your lover's drink. You will be loved for eternity.

Put on a yellow and a black garter on Easter Monday. Wear them for one year. This will ensure that you will receive a proposal. I understand that this practice is good for men as well as women. It is up to you to decide.

Think of your love as you swallow a four-leaf clover. This is a sure-fire way to get your love returned.

Make a wish with the first dove you see in springtime. The wish will then come true.

Sprinkle rose water on bay leaves. Put them on your pillow. That will help you attain your hope of dreaming of your love. (Green was the ancient Druids' symbol of hope. See chapter on Christmas wreaths and trees).

After counting 50 white horses and one white mule, the first unmarried person of the opposite sex you shake hands with will be the one you will marry.

To make sex sexier, the ancient Greeks consumed hyena udder; the eighteenth century Italian lover, Casanova, ate oysters; and the early Chinese were said to have eaten ginseng and rhinoceros horn. Present-day edibles believed to induce lust, if not love, include bananas, figs, clams, tomatoes, avocados, onions, asparagus, and the Japanese raw fish delicacy *sushi*.

OMENS ANYONE?

The first person of the opposite sex you meet on the morning of St. Valentine's Day will become your true love. So be careful.

A white dove flying overhead is said to bring good luck.

If you dream of a dove, you are promised happiness.

Most Ozark people believe that the real Ground Hog Day is on February 14th, not the 2nd. It is said they are adamant that if it is cold and cloudy on the 14th, there will be six more weeks of winter weather.

This is the best day to sow seeds, so say many Southerners.

WANT TO WIN A SWEETHEART?

Naomi Rhodes, the famous lecturer, said it all when she said, "You are always building memories." You are either building up a relationship or you are tearing it down. There is no middle ground. A still river begins to dry up.

When I say, "I love you," what I am really saying linguistically is, "When I am with you or when I think of you, I feel full of love and lovely."

Therefore, if you want someone to be your Valentine, or fall in love with you, answer this question: "What does love mean, or feel like, to your desired love?" Then, influence them to feel that way. Figure out what you can say or do to cause them to feel good when they think of you.

In the second section of Chapter IX on how to cure the holiday blues, there are scientific and systematic ways to make yourself and others feel good, such as the Keying and Cognitive Refocusing techniques. These techniques will help you to attain a mate and maintain an ongoing relationship or make it even more joyful.

If you want love, be lovable and loving. Emerson said, "Feeble souls seek to be loved, great souls seek to be lovable." We attract to us that which is in our consciousness, that which we are.

If you want love, be worthy, kind, and accepting and you will draw love worthy of you.

The best way to keep a lover loving you is to court him or her... and continue to court... and then court some more. My advice to all married couples is to remember that your courting dance enticed him or her to marry you, so never stop courting. That means, never take each other for granted and treat each other as if you are brand new lovers. Remember what you did to get each other, and do it again and again. It worked then and it will work forever.

And being insistent on "honesty as the best policy" is not always the best thing to do. The so-called "honesty" prescribed by many psychotherapists could be hostility in disguise. Be sure to know the difference. Treat your loved ones like you would your cat, if you are a cat lover. You totally accept it, you allow it absolutely independence and you laugh when it, without warning, jumps off your lap and goes elsewhere. Or, better still, treat your mate like a precious jewel, a rare blossom or a sacred gift. Your lover is the one who makes you who you are.

Forget whether or not it is going to last. There are no guarantees in life. Let go of the past, be hopeful and expectant of the future, stay in the miracle of the moment and know you are deserving of all the love you desire.

Or, you can do as our ancient ancestors did. Hide the dried tongue of a turtle dove in your prospective mate's room. This will really ensure his or her love for you forever(?).

CHAPTER III

SAINT PATRICK'S DAY

BLARNEY OR FACTS?

HAVE YOU EVER WONDERED...

... who St. Patrick really was?

... where the name came from?

... what the early spring holiday is all about?

... if he really drove the snakes out of Ireland?

... how he treated the native Druids?

... if he was really Irish or is that just more of Ireland's blarney?

... where the folklore of the Blarney Stone came from?

... what the original symbol of the shamrock meant?

... if leprechauns actually existed?

... what the shillelagh is and where it came from?

THE BLARNEY OF ST. PATRICK'S DAY

So much of St. Patrick's Day is cloaked in mystery and legend that it is hard to separate fact from blarney.

For most Irish-Americans, March 17th is both religious and festive. To the other Americans, it is best known for its rowdy, lively and festive side.

The biggest blarney of all surrounding St Patrick's Day is that this patron saint of Ireland was not Irish, but SCOTTISH!

According to Edna Barth in *Shamrocks, Harps, and Shillelaghs: The Story of the St. Patrick's Day Symbols,* his real name was Maewyn Succat. In his famous *Confession*, a collection of his own thoughts and feelings, he calls himself *patricius*, meaning well-born in Latin. He did come from a well-to-do family as his father, Calpurnius (his English name was Succat), was clever in war and an official for the Roman government.

There is controversy over exactly when he lived, but scholars conclude that it was probably around 385-460 A.D. When he was 16 years old, he was stolen from his father's Scottish farm by a band of Irish pirates and sold into slavery.

While in slavery he worked for six years as a shepherd. One day, in his solitude, he had a dream. In the dream he was told to escape and instructed how to do it. He was told to go to the sea shore two hundred miles away because a voice told him, "Thy ship is ready for thee."

After a series of adventures, including being thrown into slavery again by a band of sailors, Patrick decided to devote his life to God. He went to Europe and studied there for a few years, however no one knows where for sure. Some believe he went to France and became a monk.

On one of his rare visits to his Sottish home, he had another vision. This time he heard a voice calling him to go to Ireland and convert the *pagans*, as the non-Christians were called. These so-called pagans were actually Celts and Scandinavians who had given Ireland its original name of Irlanda.

CELTS, DRUIDS AND CULDEES

I use the term "so-called" pagans because in *Celt, Druid and Culdee,* Isabel Hill Elder shows, with a preponderance of overwhelming academic evidence, that the Druids were not a lower type of aboriginal savage, nor were they practitioners of human sacrifices. Not quite the way we read it in the history books, is it? This unworthy mental attitude was spread by the Roman war propagandists.

These ancient "pagans," and specifically the Celts, whose rites were performed by the priestly Druids, were worshipping something far more powerful than a massive hulk of stones and cement. They worshipped the Great Spirit, the Power that created nature and the earth, and they honored and revered the earth itself and everything that naturally grew upon it.

Their concept of religion was based on a very personal appreciation of life, nature and wholeness which we largely lost when we, in the western civilizations, separated ourselves from the environment over 2,000 years ago. By believing that we were bigger and better than our land and nature, and that we were able to control and manipulate our earth, we became separated and isolated not only from our earth, but also from ourselves.

Sarah Ann Osmen so eloquently summarized this in her book *Sacred Places* when she said, "Due to our conditioned separative ideas we have lost touch with that connection (with the Power) for the most part. That longing we have over the country is the longing that we have to make that connection again."

When we look closely at the massive amount of relatively hidden evidence, we find that the Celtic Druids, often called "Magi," were required to study for a lengthy twenty years to master the complete Druidic knowledge (their "Ph.D." so to speak).

Their scholastic endeavors included knowledge in natural philosophy, astronomy, mathematics, geometry, medicine, jurisprudence, poetry and oratory. Natural philosophy and astronomy had reached an incredibly high level of sophistication. It is these giants of intellect and deep spirituality to whom we owe more than 90% of all our holiday symbols and customs except for Thanksgiving, and there it is about 50%. We also owe a great deal of acknowledgment to the Celtic priests for the attitudes we hold toward political and religious freedom.

The Druids were responsible for having built roads centuries before the Romans landed on the Isles. They were called the "Kings Highways." These were the roads on which the butchering Romans drove their chariots into Briton in 43 A.D. Because of the Celts' faith and tenacity to hold on, it was only after 10 years of attempting to enter that the Romans ever actually set foot on the Druids' land.

The Celtic Druids, and later the Culdees, were a part of the first Christian Church outside of Jerusalem. The evidence is overwhelming and irrefutable that some apostles, perhaps St. Peter and St. Paul, and over twenty thousand Christians escaped Rome and its persecutions during the first century, landed in the Britons, and created the first Christian Church there.

So, by St. Patrick's time, it is thought by various historians, Christianity had been introduced to Ireland three and a half centuries earlier and many of the Irish were already Christians. Patrick was not the first Christian in Ireland. Perhaps some more Irish blarney.

In fact, St. Patrick, according to Elder, belonged to the Culdee Church when he began his work as a missionary revivalist. That is why Edna Barth stated that "Patrick never tried to stamp out old Irish rites and customs. Instead, he found a way to combine them with Christian customs. The Irish had always honored their gods with spring fire rites, for example. So Patrick had the people gather outside the churches for Easter bonfires."

It is an intriguing play of history to note that the Christian Church in Ireland, as founded by Patrick, existed for about 700 years free and unshackled and maintained its independence. It had no connection with England, and differed on important points from the Roman Church.

However, history tell us that eventually it fell to obedience to the Roman Pontiff because of the intrigues of Henry II and the Pope in 1172. But all was not lost because, in the Church's true fashion,

Patrick was declared a saint in order to keep the Irish people calm and under control.

All of the great historians, such as Pliny and Tacitus, Strabo, Mathew Arnold and Max Muller, told of how, up to the 4th or 5th century, it was the massacring, plundering Romans who were absorbed by the Druidic culture, not the other way around.

The Roman Church, around 600 A.D., after having lost its foothold in any political power, began its attempt at the final annihilation of the British Christian Church which had been in existence for over 500 years. Neither the Roman Church nor the Romans ever succeeded completely.

Be that as it may, the Druids and the first Christians were scholars. The Romans, as it turned out, were the true barbarians. The Druids were judges and lawyers. Their law is believed to have been derived from Semitic and Hebrew law. They were scientists. They developed the telescope and, probably, that is why they were attributed with the magical powers of being able to bring the moon into the palm of one's hand.

The true superstitions and lies were propagated by the Romans and later by the Roman Church in order to pillage the Druids' tin, gold, enamelled art and products of their rich commerce. These acts of greed were done, not by the so-called pagans (the Druids and the Culdian Christians who believed in one Supreme Being), but rather by the true pagans, the Romans who worshipped many gods.

It is not my intent to sound anti-Catholic because of the history I am reporting. Nor do I think we should we kill the message because of the various messengers. Many of the old "pagan" customs and symbols still prevail in various sections throughout the world and the United States. And because of that, I believe we should happily acknowledge our ancient ancestors with a feeling of deep gratitude.

We cannot, and should not, destroy some of the fears, phobias and folklores we have inherited from our past, because our sixth sense tells us that we march on a path, or a wisdom, that we have inherited. Osman concludes that the so-called mysteries of the Druidic past, as well as Norse mythology, were truly a matter of accepting the mystery of the universe and the feeling of this power through the presence of sensual objects. It was their religiousness. Everything in their environment was sacred because everything pointed to Divinity.

During the pre-Christian era, the Druids, in fact the Celts through all of Briton, believed that people were as much of an element of earth's wholeness as were the plants and animals of the earth.

The Druid priests held ceremonies in sacred oak groves and foretold the future. Each chieftain in Ireland had his own Druid priest to give advice and protection by means of magic. Magic at that time was in reality the science of the day and was not of the supernatural as we think of it today.

"Some of the superstitious practices and magical spells seem irrational or at least have irrational explanations and," says Sarah Ann Osmen, "the irrationality is nothing more than the presently unexplained." She goes on to say that what is irrational to us may have been clearly and wholly understandable to our ancient ancestors.

I am not saying that the superstitions are necessarily true. However, we must not close our minds and arbitrarily rule out the possibility that because of the energies that have been attributed to particular ideas and customs, they have been deeply ingrained in our culture. Scientist Stephan Schwartz suggests that perhaps because of the intensity of the energy that has been devoted, the determination and the repetitiveness may, in fact, create a sacredness that we now wish to understand. He calls that critical mass of energy "numinosity." Carl Jung suggests a "collective unconscious," Sarah Osman proposes "noosphere," and Rubert Sheldrake hints at a "morphogenetic field." Whatever the name, the fact is, sacred places, ideas and customs persist with unbelievable tenacity.

I was struck when I found, to my utter fascination, very little contradiction between the Christian beliefs and the Druid beliefs that God, or the Heavenly Spirit, the Creator of all reality, completely surrounds us and exists in all things. A pantheistic God, perhaps, but an all loving, all caring and all prevailing God.

Today, St. Patrick's Day is the occasion for the biggest annual parade held in New York City and is celebrated throughout the country by practically all of us in one way or another. This is the day when "everybody is Irish!"

THE WEARIN' O' THE GREEN

As we all know, most holidays have their special colors. Christmas gleams with red and green; St. Valentine's Day has its red and pink; Halloween is known for black and orange. St. Patrick's Day is clothed in the color of Ireland, a refreshing green.

"Long before St. Patrick," Barth writes, "the green of grass, of shamrocks, and of all growing things had special meaning to the Irish. It was a symbol of springtime." At this time of the year, like other people of ancient times, the Celtic Druids honored, but not necessarily worshiped, the gods and goddesses of plant life, especially the plants that stayed green all year long. They were considered a symbol of hope and eternal life. Green has always been considered the symbol of hope in the language of colors.

Then with the coming of St. Patrick and other missionaries, some of the old pagan rites became linked to important days in the Christian calendar. Gradually, the pagan springtime celebratism was replaced by St. Patrick's Day and Easter.

SHAMROCK LORE

In Irish history, the shamrock is the best known and most popular of all the symbols of the Irish holiday.

Holidays have their own special symbols as well as colors. As we all know, Halloween greets us with the grinning Jack-o-lantern. Christmas is wrapped in a red bow and decorated with holly and mistletoe. St. Valentines Day is welcomed with Cupid, bow and arrows and piercing hearts. There is one symbol that says it all for St. Patrick's Day, and that is the green shamrock, a small three-leaved plant that looks like our three-leaved clover.

The shamrock has been an emblem of St. Patrick as well as of Ireland for centuries. The shamrock is also found combined with the English rose and the Scottish thistle, on the coat of arms of Great Britain.

Called *seamrog* in Gaelic, the shamrock's true identity has been debated. According to Barth, "an Englishman once claimed that it was the wood sorrel. A loyal Irishman wrote a letter to the newspaper, the *Dublin Penny Journal,* and called the wood sorrel 'that sour, puny plant' and the Irish shamrock 'our little darling.' The same man claimed that when St. Patrick drove the snakes out of Ireland, he was standing in a patch of shamrock."

The four-leafed clover should not be confused with the shamrock. However the number four draws most of its power from a mystical connotation. In numerology and mythology, the number appears constantly as a symbol of balance, unity and absoluteness. The four-leafed clover's comparative rarity helps to give it an aura of good fortune.

We all know that it is the shamrock's three-leaved shape that has also become a symbol of good luck. Bishop Patrick used it as a metaphor when teaching about the *trinity* of the Catholic faith, the Father, Son and Holy Ghost.

THE MAGIC OF THREE FOR LUCK

Scholars speculate that the number three has always been important and may have come from the wonder that our ancient ancestors had about the birth mystery. They observed two humans or two animals, who, after mating, created a third entity. It must have been looked upon as something magical and supernatural.

The number three was not original to St. Patrick's time. It was considered unique in religions far older. Three was the number of the Druids' unknown god. In ancient Rome, Jupiter, Neptune and Pluto, the gods of the heavens, seas and the earth, respectively, were believed to be the three godly rulers of the world.

The Three Graces and the Three Fates depicted the magical number of Greek mythology. Pythagoras is said to have believed that the number three had a beginning, a middle, and an end, and was a symbol of completeness.

With the long history of symbolism of the number three, it is not surprising to find it in the Christian religion as well as fairy tales and folklore. For everyone knows of the three sisters and three wishes.

And we are aware of the old folklore saying about the number three. "Three's a Charm," and "Never two without three."

The Irish use the Shamrock, like many people use the Key, to create various physical feelings. Keying, is explained in the second part of Chapter IX on Christmas holiday blues.

SNAKES AND ST. PATRICK: TRUTH OR MORE BLARNEY?

One of the most well-known acts attributed to St. Patrick was that he got rid of the snakes. He is often shown in pictures, holding a shamrock, in the act of ostracizing the snakes.

An old Irish legend, according to Barth, "tells of one stubborn serpent who refused to go. Making a box, St. Patrick invited the serpent to get inside. 'It's too small for me,' said the serpent.

'No, indeed,' said St. Patrick. 'It's just right for you.' They argued some more. Then the serpent said, 'I still say it's too small, and I'll prove it.' With that, he climbed into the box; St. Patrick slammed down the lid and heaved the whole thing into the ocean."

In another legend, St. Patrick beat a drum to run the snakes out of Ireland. However, he knocked a hole in the drum, because he beat a little too hard. But, because he was in a holy act, it was mended for him quickly by an angel.

I enjoy the legend that claims that St. Patrick magically made the Irish soil so repugnant that a serpent would die if he even touched it. The eighth century English scholar, Bede, went even further. He said that when a snake got the first whiff of Irish air he would die.

Some scholars suggest that the reason that St. Patrick is given credit for getting rid of snakes and toads in Ireland is that, to the invading Norsemen from Scandinavia, the name "Patrick" sounded like their word *paudrid,* "the expeller of toads." However when they got there, they found no snakes and decided that Paudrig must have expelled them along with the toads.

It might be well to note that biologists have assured us that there really were no snakes and very few toads in Ireland prior to and during Patrick's time.

THE SHILLELAGH

The Irish name *shillelagh* means a stout oak club or cudgel. "A sprig of shillelagh" originally came from the famous oak forest called Shillelagh. The early Irish used the shillelagh as a walking stick and a weapon. But, when fighting, they used two. Nowadays, with the absent of oak, the walking stick is made of blackthorn hedge.

LEPRECHAUNS

The Irish have all kinds of fairies, one of which, the leprechaun, is seen as a tiny shoemaker. Barth says that usually he is wearing a green suit and cap and is one of a whole horde of Irish fairies. Trooping fairies were kind, loving, pleasant and traveled in groups, while the solitary fairies who lived alone, like the leprechauns, "were mostly mean and spiteful." This says something about the values of living with someone!

In ancient times they were a part of a group known as *luchorpans* (the wee ones) and were probably part of the "little people" legends.

FAIRIES

According to Barth, the Irish were always in awe of their fairies. She said, "They believed that fairies sometimes kidnapped brides and snatched babies from their cradles. A person enticed into a fairy mound might be kept there for a hundred years, they thought. Listening to fairy music could make a man or woman lose all sense of human care or joy. Forever afterward, he or she would seem to live in another world. Such a person might become a seer, a great poet, or musician." Legend has it that O'Carolan, the famous harpist, created his tunes while sleeping on a fairy mound. These fairy mounds, some scholars think, could have been ancient forts or small gardens of the "little people." (See Halloween chapter for more on the "little people)

Some of the fairy mounds, she went on to say, "can still be seen in Ireland to this day. And many Irish farmers will not disturb them any more than they will interfere with trees or paths that are thought to belong to fairies."

Are the fairies real? Some suggest that when belief in the Christian God became prevalent, the ancient gods were retained as tiny beings in the minds of the people.

The leprechaun, however, is the only fairy in Irish lore to have a place in St. Patrick's Day. Why? Scholars believe it may be because of his green clothing but, paradoxically, that was intended to make him hard to be detected.

The fat-bellied little old man dressed in green that we see as a souvenir or on a greeting card is part leprechaun and part farmer, a contrived symbol of the holiday. More blarney?

BLARNEY AND THE BLARNEY STONE

The word *blarney* means cajolery; the gift of a cajoling tongue. When used as a verb, it means to cajole, wheedle or tatter. Perhaps the use of blarney is where the saying, "Oh, you're full of bologna!" originally came from.

Legend has it that whoever kisses the *Blarney Stone*, says *Funk and Wagnalls Standard Dictionary of Folklore, Mythology and Legend*, "'will never want for words;' forever after he possesses a cajoling tongue and the gift of skillful lying without detection."

The stone is presently set in a high fenced-off area of the Blarney Castle built by Cormac McCarthy in the 15th century, located in the village of Blarney, County Cork, Ireland.

The origin of the powers of the stone is related in an ancient Irish legend found in *Funk and Wagnalls*. The legend says that the magic in the stone was revealed to Cormac McCarthy by the infamous folk-lore banshee, Cliodna (Cleena) herself. In old Irish mythology, Cliodna was the daughter of Gebann, the chief Druidic priest to Manannan Mac Lir, the lord of the sea. She was similar to the Greek Circe, the seducer of sailors who sent ships blindly to the rocks of destruction.

The Blarney Stone story tells of when Cormac was worried about a lawsuit, but Cliodna told him, "Kiss the stone you come face to face with in the morning, and the proper words will pour out of you." So when Cormac woke, he walked forth and kissed the stone and the words just poured out of him. He won the lawsuit. (Note: Perhaps, all successful attorneys and talk show hosts have kissed the Blarney Stone.)

Distressed again, but this time about the possibility that every one in Ireland would come to kiss the stone, and would get in trouble with such slippery speech, Cormac took it where it is today.

Today, it is at the top of the castle, surrounded with an iron grating to safeguard the visitors and is hard to get to. To kiss it, you must hang upside while doing the kissing.

YOU OL' COOT!

This is not blarney. *Clootie* comes from *coot*, one side of a cleft hoof, and is the Scotsmen's term for the devil. *You Old Coot* is a variant. *Clootie's Croft is* a piece of land left as a gift to the devil because it is not possible to cultivate it.

PHOBIAS SURROUNDING ST. PATRICKS'S DAY

Phobias and stress that are generally associated with some of the other holidays are not found around St.Patrick's Day. Only on rare occasions are there reports of people with excessive fear and stress on this day.

There are uncommon incidents where a person will suffer from *ophidophobia*, the extreme fearfulness of snakes. Even more infrequently will someone have enough fearful symptoms to be considered having *chromatophobia*, the fear of colors or the color green. Many people do suffer from *ochilophobia*, the fear of crowds, and even more have *phonophopbia*, the fear of loud noises and loud yelling. However these people usually stay away from the parades and parties and get along fairly well as the celebration passes.

Curiously, there has never been one reported incident of *mythophobia* among the Irish. That is the fear of making false statements. Perhaps, they have all, by osmosis, kissed the Blarney Stone.

PREDICTIONS, OMENS AND RITUALS

For good luck in love, throw nine straight willow rods towards the rafters of the house and catch them coming down. However, you must, while doing this, stand on one leg with one hand behind your back.

Find a four-leafed clover and you will have good luck.

Find a four-leafed clover on St. Patrick's Day and you will have double, double good luck.

If you are a single female and find a four-leafed clover, hang it over the door, and the first bachelor you meet you will marry.

Wear something green and eat something green on St. Patrick's Day and that will bring you good luck.

To make cabbage seeds grow better, sow them while wearing your nightclothes on March 17th. As with many superstitions, if not most, there is a trace of pagan fertility rite in this one. Through sympathetic magic, the performance of the sexual act will help the cabbage seeds to germinate. It is up to you whether you let your mate in on what you are up to.

Kill a snake on St. Patrick's Day and you will have bad luck. Seems like it should be the other way around, but you know the Irish.

To cure a headache, wear the rattles of a rattlesnake. If it does not cure yours, it certainly will the snake's.

Rheumatism can be cured, or prevented, by carrying with you the ashes of a burnt toad.

The old English lore for ridding yourself of warts is to hang a live toad in a bag around your neck. Others think that just the leg will do the job.

If you are prone to stealing, keep a dried heart of a toad with you at all times to prevent being detected.

To increase your psychic ability, listen to some fairy music.

Do not disturb the mounds of the "little people" on March 17. It will bring bad luck.

This one was used on leprechauns, but it might work with children. Tell them that a silver dollar is under one of the weeds in the back yard and it is theirs to go find.

So on St. Patrick's Day, enjoy the day as it has come to be, a day of parades, joy and festivities. Wear your green, watch out for the leprechauns and the ol' coot with the shillelagh, and have fun. Remember, this is the day when "everybody is Irish!"

CHAPTER IV

FRIDAY THE 13TH

PARASKEVIDEKATRIAPHOBIA - Do You Have It?

FOLKLORE AND PHOBIAS - BELIEF VERSUS SUPERSTITION

HAVE YOU EVER WONDERED...

... why the number of members in occult, mystical and esoteric movements is on the rise?

... what the reason is for the soaring number of superstitions, obsessive/ compulsive rituals and phobias surrounding Friday the 13th?

... if it is because of some satanic crusade or is there a more scientific explanation?

... how our industries, the American government and the U.S. Armed Services are effected by Friday the 13th?

... why the fear of the number 13 is deeply rooted in our history?

... how Friday became the "bad" day of the week and not Monday?

... who started this fear of the number "13" anyway? Was it some dysfunctional Roman family, an alcoholic Norseman or a drug induced Druid?

... how Adam and Eve got into the picture of fear of Friday the 13th?

... how fear of the number 13 is being constantly reinforced?

... what the difference is between superstitions, beliefs and phobias?

... what effect the economy has on superstitions and phobias?

... hat the symptoms are of paraskevidekatriaphobia?

... if the sufferers should seek psychological help?

... if people can actually become addicted to fear and unhappiness?

... what some psychological suggestions are for handling these fears?

... if all superstitions are negative?

... what good things have happened on Friday the 13th?

... what some ancient folklore "cures" are that deal with fear of Friday the 13th?

... if walking around your house 13 times really does ward off evil spirits or is chewing a piece of beef gristle while standing on your head better?

PARASKEVIDEKATRIAPHOBIA?

When Friday the 13th looms, it brings high anxiety for "paraskevidekatriaphobiacs!" No, that's not some long extinct horned and winged creature from the Mesozoic age. Paraskevidekatriaphobiacs -- whew -- are people with blind unreasoning fear about the day Friday and the number thirteen, as opposed to those who have a clear, reasonable fear of not being able to say that word.

If Friday the 13th is threatening and bothersome to you, you may be suffering from a case of PARASKEVIDEKATRIAPHOBIA! I jokingly tell my patients, "When you learn to pronounce it, you're cured!"

Historically, "triskaidekaphobia" means the fear of Friday the 13th, but that term means only "the fear of the number 13." "Friday" is not even in the word. The term, "Paraskevidekatriaphobia," which I coined circa 1982, is the true word for the combined fear of the day Friday and the number 13.

All of us are affected, feel a little edgy, or at least have some funny thoughts about the number 13 and the day Friday. Psychologists have found that when they are joined on a Friday the 13th, there are millions of people who have paralyzing fear and go through all sorts of rituals to counteract the harmful effects. Dr. Arthur Hardy, a psychiatrist and phobia expert of Menlo Park, California, has been quoted as estimating that approximately 10 million people in the United States alone suffer from some form of fear of Friday the 13th. However, I believe that his figures are somewhat low. Based on observations at the Phobia Institute over the past 10 years, it would be more accurate to say that it is between 17 to 21 million Americans.

Statistics extrapolated from Douglas Hill's estimates, in his book *Magic and Superstition,* indicate that Friday the 13th costs the United States over $750,000,000.00 (that's over 750 **million** dollars) in lost business --- because, when possible, people will stay at home rather then shop, travel or go out and take risks of any kind.

Although Friday the 13th is not a genuine holiday, in the official sense, it does cause a lot of commotion. Because of its erratic schedule of appearances every year, there will never be fewer than one nor more than three days on which Friday the 13th falls, and there is no particular month in which it creates its excitement. Also, it lacks any specific customs, symbols or practices like those found with the more authentic holidays, such as Halloween, Valentine's Day, or Christmas.

But, as you will see, there is no lack of legends, folklore, "remedies" and excitement about its origins.

HOW IS THE FEAR OF FRIDAY THE 13TH PERPETUATED?

The superstitions and folklore surrounding the number thirteen and the day Friday are much more ingrained in our society than we can, at first, imagine. It is fascinating how fear of the number 13 is constantly reinforced by happenings around us and how industry, the government and the armed services have been and are effected by Friday the 13th.

No voyage, according to ancient maritime tradition, should begin on a Friday because sailors believed that bad luck would fall on all. Douglas Hill, in his book, *Magic and Superstitions,* relates the story that Lord Byron, it is said, purposefully attempted to defy this belief by sailing for Greece on a Friday, and died in that country.

As recently as the late 1800's, the belief that merchant ships sailing on Friday the 13th were doomed was so widespread that the famous insurance company, Lloyds of London, refused to insure any ship sailing on that date.

Sailors still tell of the ship-owners who set out to discredit the taboo. They laid the keel of a ship on a Friday and named the ship after the day. They gave the command to a captain named Friday and sent the ship on its maiden voyage on a Friday. The ship never reached port and was never seen or heard from again.

In years past, ocean liners scheduled to leave port on the 13th (Friday or not) would often contrive to delay their departures until after midnight. I experienced this when I was in the U.S. Navy, not so long ago, and heard rumors of attempts to delay setting out to sea on a Friday or on the thirteenth.

Even today, the U.S. Navy will not launch a ship on Friday the 13th. And there are many people who simply won't do any traveling of any kind on that day.

Funk & Wagnalls Standard Dictionary of Folklore, Mythology and Legend summarizes that it is bad luck to be born or get married on a Friday. It is bad luck to take a new job on a Friday, cut one's nails on a Friday, or visit the sick on a Friday. If you turn your bed on a Friday, you will not sleep. Criminals expect a hard sentence if they are unlucky enough to be tried on a Friday.

If you want to use folklore to beat the weather forecaster's percentages, just remember that "Wet Friday, wet Sunday," is a common saying in general weather lore.

According to an Associated Press poll reported in USA TODAY, February, 26, 1992, two in five people believe that U.S. built cars built on Fridays have more mechanical problems because workers become careless.

Rick Horowitz, in the 1987 *Old Farmer's Almanac,* stated in the article "Have a Happy Friday the 13th" that the town fathers of French Lick Springs, Indiana, not long ago decreed that all black cats in town should wear bells on Friday the 13th.

Want a great job? French socialites known as "quatorziens" ("fourteeners") once made themselves available as emergency fill-ins when the guest list for a dinner party unexpectedly contained 13 names.

Many theater managers, as well as many employees, will not open a new show on a Friday and especially on Friday the 13th.

Ballplayers often feel it is bad luck to play on a Friday.

Recently we have had threats of computer viruses scaring the wits out of the data processing industry on Friday the 13th.

Many businessmen dislike starting a new venture, beginning a business trip or signing contracts on the 13th or on a Friday.

The Otis Elevator Company reports that about 90 percent of our skyscrapers, and many big hotels, have no 13th floor.

Hospitals, hotels and similar institutions, often have no rooms numbered thirteen.

Universal Studios, in Southern California, has no studios with the number 13 on them.

Many airlines and sports arenas omit 13 as a seat number. Some airports, as in Fresno, California, do not use 13 as a gate number.

Many people in certain parts of the world still find it hard to have 13 as a house number. They have 12 1/2 instead. In many streets and squares in Florence, Italy, 12 1/2 substitutes for 13. In France, to replace the number 12, they use twelve twice, as in 1212.

So we can see that customs in our culture constantly reinforce the fear of the day Friday and the number thirteen, alone and combined. And this fear surfaces in the daily lives of millions of Paraskavidekatriaphobiacs who suffer varying degrees of mental and physical symptoms. Many perform rituals, over which they have no control, to counteract their fear.

WHY ALL THE FUSS?

Why did Friday become the "bad" day of the week and not Monday?

Superstition has been with us since the days of the cave man. We're all aware of folklore sayings like "Don't walk under a ladder," "Spit three times over your shoulder," and "Step on a crack, break your mother's back." While some of us laugh or pay no attention to these superstitions, there are millions among us who live their lives with hundreds of little rituals designed to ward off evil and protect themselves from whatever it is they fear on Friday the 13th.

But why Friday, and why the number 13 instead of, say, 17?

Let us take a look at the number thirteen first, then Friday, and then the combination of the two.

Scholars say that the fear of the number 13 is rooted deeply in ancient history. Today most people think that "triskaidekaphobia," the fear of the number thirteen, came out of the fact that thirteen sat down at the Last Supper but, in fact, the superstition is far older.

One early anthropological theory is that primitive people were only comfortable with what they could clearly see and terrified at what the could not see or understand. These early ancients counted with their ten fingers and two feet and this allowed them to count only to 12. After 12 came the unknown. Remember, it is only a theory, as all of these are.

The ancient Greeks and Romans disliked the number thirteen in their numerological fortune-telling because they regarded it as a sign of destruction.

Also, in early Rome witches gathered in groups of twelve, and the thirteenth member was believed to be the devil. In slightly more recent times, the number has continued to have unpleasant associations; in the days of witch hunts, the witches' covens were supposedly composed of thirteen members.

According to Hill, Norse mythology tells of an ancient legend where there were twelve gods gathered for a dinner party when the thirteenth, a mischievous and cruel semi-god, Loki, the red-haired evildoer and spirit of strife, sneaked in uninvited. Once there, he tricked a blind god to kill Balder the Beautiful, the god of joy and gladness, the favorite of the gods and of the world. Balder was killed by the blind god, Hoder, the god of darkness, with a javelin made from mistletoe. (Later in the chapter on Christmas we will see why we must kiss while under the mistletoe.)

When the beautiful Balder (Baldur,) the god of joy and gladness fell dead, darkness fell throughout the universe and the whole earth mourned according to Magnus Magnusson in his book *Hammer of the North*. From that moment on, the number thirteen has been considered ominous and foreboding.

For mythical reasons, the ancient Vikings considered the number thirteen unlucky and their hangman's noose contained thirteen knots. In fact, to this day a there are thirteen knots in a properly knotted hangman's noose and there are thirteen steps up to the gallows. Unlucky for some, to be sure.

In the Christian Biblical references, as we know, at the Last Supper there were thirteen attending, including Judas who betrayed Jesus.

Friday, as well as the number 13, has been considered ominous for centuries. Scholars have noted that it is an unlucky day, in general, in most European folk belief also. The reasons are manifold.

Some folklorian scholars believe that our friend, the Norse god Balder, was killed not only by the uninvited thirteenth guest, Loki, but on a Friday as well.

Although it has little to do with Friday being an unlucky day, Friday is the day of the Nordic goddess Frigga. According to *Funk & Wagnalls,* Frigga, Frigg, Frija, or Fri in Teutonic mythology, after whom our day Friday is named, is the second and principal wife of Odin, the father of all gods. She is the mother of our good friend Balder, the god of goodness.

Even though she shared the throne with Odin, most of her time was spent in her own home *Fensalir.* When she was not spinning golden thread or multicolored clouds, she looked after mortals by smoothing the path of lovers, both single and married, and dispensing wisdom and justice through her eleven handmaidens.

In apocryphal writings, Fridays are thought to be as equally unlucky as the number thirteen. Ancient manuscripts imply that it all started when Eve gave Adam the apple to eat. Supposedly, that infamous day fell on a Friday and many scholars believe it was on Friday the 13th. I have absolutely no idea how this was deduced or which calendar was being used!

Friday, and the 13th specifically, is also thought by many to be the day when Cain slew his brother Abel. The crucifixion, as we know, fell on a Friday and, during the days of the Druids, Friday was the night of the "Witches' Sabbath."

We can see that when the ominous backdrop of the number thirteen is combined with the foreboding history of the day Friday, we find a picture of Friday the 13th as the most heinous and sinister day of the year in Western civilization. And has been for centuries.

WHY THE RISE IN OCCULT
AND MYSTICAL MOVEMENTS?

Reviewing economic indicators and periodicals, researchers Vernon Padgett and Dale Jorgenson looked for popular interest in astrology and mysticism during periods of high unemployment and economic and social instability. Under this anxiety and stress they found quite simply that economic "threat produces superstition." They reported in the "Personality and Social Psychology Bulletin" (Vol. 8, No 4) that as unemployment increased and wages and indus-

trial production fell, articles about astrology and mysticism prolifer-
ated.

In *The Authoritarian Personality,* sociologist T. W. Adorno reports from his classic study that "superstition thrives on economic
instability." I think it would be better to say that with any kind anxiety, stress or threat, the thrust toward superstitious beliefs and behavior is increased in any population.

The historical mass movement into the cities which has crowded
people together more than ever has resulted in increased air, water
and food pollution. Violent crime has never been so widespread. The
resultant stress is at an all time high. Stress and fear are exactly the
same in the body.

We have all heard of the study which found that when mice were
crowded together, they would begin to manifest aberrant behavior. In
addition to crazy actions, the mice's immune systems were negatively
effected. They got sick, had heart attacks, developed cancers and died
younger than the control group who had plenty of space.

Those reasons, I believe, are why we have, at the Phobia Institute
as well as elsewhere, seen a rise in the interest in the occult, mystical
and esoteric movements. It is not because of some satanic crusade.
There is, thank goodness, a more scientific explanation. It is because
of the extreme societal stressors the world is experiencing.

Not only have we seen an increased interest in the occult because
of the excessive stressors, of economic and social unrest, but they
also explain, and are connected with, the soaring number of superstitions, obsessive/compulsive rituals and phobias surrounding Friday
the 13th. Seventeen to twenty million Americans suffer from some
sort of symptoms which range from mild to extremely severe.

WHAT ARE THE SYMPTOMS OF
PARASKEVIDEKATRIAPHOBIA?

To the sufferers of paraskevidekatriaphobia, the difference between superstitions, beliefs and phobias is hardly discernable, and
they often can become addicted to the fearful feelings. Like any other
addict, they are addicted in terms of being out of control of their

thoughts, feelings and actions while still not wanting the horrible experience.

The symptoms of paraskevidekatriaphobia can range from slight nervous giggles and mild anxiety to the excessive fear and actual physical reactions of a full blown panic attack. The indications include hyperventilation, lightheadedness, dizziness and rapid heartbeat. This can bring on the additional fear of having a heart attack.

Some start getting the symptoms a week or two before the actual day, while others suffer from severe anxiety only on the day itself. One young man in his twenties would not even get out of bed for fear that something evil would befall him.

Any Friday the 13th talk show on which I have appeared, either as a guest or as the host, has received calls from many people reporting that they are unable to leave their homes because of the fear of something awful happening that day.

Some people will go through all sorts of obsessive/compulsive rituals to counteract the effects. I once treated a 32 year old male patient who would go through all sorts of ritualistic behavior before leaving his house for work on Friday the 13th. He would lock and unlock his front door exactly eight times and then walk around his home three times before he felt comfortable enough to drive to work. The number of times he required himself to do certain things did not seem to have any folklore or mythical significance. However, he was compelled to perform the ritual every Friday the 13th.

Another patient, a working mother of two whom I treated on the telephone home treatment program, had to walk around her car exactly three times before she would get in and drive from her home on Friday the 13th. Again, to her the number of times had no mystical or religious importance.

There are millions of people in the United States who suffer from these and other such symptoms.

DO THE SUFFERERS NEED PSYCHOLOGICAL HELP?

People who are superstitious about Friday the 13th are not more likely to be mentally ill than those who do not share that fear. Superstitions, beliefs in the occult, and religion cut across all social, economic and intellectual boundaries. And often, one person's belief is another's superstition.

Even people with some of the above symptoms should be very cautious about going to a psychiatrist, psychologist or counselor unless he or she is an expert in the field of phobias and anxiety disorders. As I said in my book, *Keying: The Power of Positive Feelings, Overcoming Fears, Phobias and Stress*, psychotherapy, as it is often practiced, can be detrimental to your mental, emotional and physical health. Psychotherapy is not predictably effective and when it is, the results, more often than not, do not last.

Why is therapy considered dangerous? As I discuss in detail elsewhere in this book (and as developed by authors R. Laing, D. Chopra, J. Haley, J. Hillman, G. Wood, T. Szasz, D. Jackson and others), traditional psychotherapy tends to go back into the past, and talk about the problem and hunt for possible "root causes." This digging into the hurtful past creates physical feelings that are associated with the problem. And they are bad, negative feelings. As I have said many times, "What you think about you begin to feel, what you feel generates what you do, and what you do creates how you will become." If you talk about horrible things, you will begin to feel horrible feelings.

When you practice a part in a play or repeat, over and over, a piece on the piano, or any musical instrument, you become more proficient at it. That is called rehearsal, and practice makes permanence. Generally, people have rehearsed their phobic feelings so often, and so well, that they do not need any more of that. That is why talk therapy can be so detrimental.

Pharmacological treatments, that is drug therapy, also have their deleterious draw backs. Bad side-effects are often exactly the same as the symptoms being treated. When this happens, the treating practitioner could be treating the side-effects and not the real symptoms.

Therefore, to repeat, it is imperative that the practitioner must, for safety sake, be a specialist in the field of anxiety disorders, and specifically phobias. A specialist will be able to tell not only what is wrong, but specifically, how he or she is going to treat it, how long it will take, (within two or three weeks,) and specifically how much it is going to cost. If they cannot do those things, then they are not an expert. Do not hire them.

Persons suffering from anxiety and phobias have not lost their minds, but have simply lost control of their minds. There is a big difference. People should realize that they have learned behaviors, including anxieties and phobias, and to unlearn them is very easy when counseled by an expert who specializes in phobias and anxiety disorders. In Chapter IX, Part II on curing the holiday blues, a scientifically proven, step-by-step program will be covered which will wash away anxieties and phobias easily, predictably and permanently.

Some of the current practices in treating people with phobias and anxieties are less effective than some of the tongue-in-cheek folklore cures that will follow.

WHO WERE THE EARLIEST SCIENTISTS?

Helpless before the forces of nature, people interpreted these unknown powers as being gods. Then humans could attempt to influence the gods to grant their desires, but whatever resulted was the will of the gods. So the shamans, witch doctors and sorcerers came into being to answer questions about their world, to make order out of it and to attempt to control the gods.

In fact, early "scientists" were people who, 10 to 20 thousand years ago, practiced magic and sorcery. Witches (which comes from the Saxon word "Wica" and means the "Wise One") and magicians served in this capacity. Later, in the chapter about the folklore of Christmas, we will see that our word "magic" comes from the term "Magi," also meaning the wise ones.

Later in our history, "priests" of various religions were assigned the job of interpreting nature and the will of God, explaining our world and helping to control our destiny through various divination practices and prayers.

Later still, came the "scientists" who were the ones with the magic of knowing what the earth and the beings in it were all about. Their myth was built around what scholars call "the superstition of materiality." They were the scientists as we know them today. They followed the "scientific" model and were the Newtons, Galileos and Einsteins. Physics, and now quantum physics, fall into this category.

Then, finally, a new breed was born: "behavioral scientists." These new interpreters of our world are called psychiatrists and psychologists. They hide behind the guise of the "scientific model" attempting to explain human and animal nature. The only problem is that their "science," as is all science, is smothered in a multitude of theories, practically none of which are predictably verifiable. Yet they have taken on the job of helping people and explaining how the world works through various private practices. Some are "private" for obvious reasons and border on the occult. Occult means to "hide" or "to keep secret," and much information has been or is "hidden" to protect the powers of the "scientist." This hiding of information has not changed much with some religious beliefs as well.

A GOOD LUCK FRIDAY?

In Irish folk belief says that it is good to die on Friday, be buried on Saturday, and get prayed for on Sunday.

Good luck for Igor Secorsky who is known for inventing the helicopter on Friday, September 13, 1939.

Whether Friday the 13th is considered lucky or unlucky depends on how you view it. As Richard Horowitz in the 1987 *Old Farmer's Almanac*, said, "As with so many things, where you stand depends on where you sit." For example, on Friday the 13th of July in 1900, Teddy Roosevelt laid the cornerstone for a new county courthouse in New York and spoke of the need for honesty and decency in government. "During the exercises," a newspaper reported the next day that "Nathaniel Ketcham, who was on the platform, had his pockets picked for $140, another for $103 and several watches were stolen."

It was a good day for people who like courthouses and thieves, but not such a good day for Nathaniel Ketcham.

Francis Scott Key wrote "The Star Spangled Banner" on September 13, 1814—very good luck for us unless you were unfortunate enough to hear Roseane Barr at the ball game. And on that same date in 1857, Milton S. Hershey, candy-maker, was born. That was good luck for the spellmakers of love (see St. Valentine's Day, Chapter II). Hershey also died on a 13th in October of 1945.

All in all, the 13th has a mixed record, historically speaking. Still, some people just don't take very kindly to it. The Turks, it is said, almost erased the number from their vocabulary.

In Madagascar the unlucky number is six. In Japan it is three. But in China the numbers three and nine (which is three times three), are considered very lucky indeed.

Then there are those who consider the number 13 quite lucky, like in Great Britain. Horowitz says that "there, by eating Christmas pudding in 13 different houses before January 1 is supposed to bring joy and prosperity in the next year." President Eisenhower was lucky, too; he was even made honorary president of Missouri's Lucky 13 Club, consisting of that state's 13 presidential electorates. They liked the fact that "Ike Eisenhower" had 13 letters."

In fact, the U.S.A. is so full of lucky 13ths that even normally superstitious political types should put their minds at ease, he went on to say. George Washington laid the cornerstone for the White House on a 13th (October 1792). The cornerstone for the Supreme Court was laid on the same date in 1932. There were 13 original colonies, of course, and the Great Seal.

The United States Seal, ignoring the omen, contains no fewer than 8 groups of 13, representing the original 13 States. It contains two 13 letter Latin mottoes: *E Pluribus Unum* which means "From many, one" *and Annuit coeptis which* means "He has favored our undertaking." Symbols on the back of that seal represent the 13 colonies and include a 13-star constellation above the eagle's head along with 13 arrows, and an olive branch with 13 leaves and 13 olives held in the eagle's claws. All of them epitomize how lucky we are to live here.

ANCIENT FOLKLORE "CURES" AND SUPERSTITIOUS PRESCRIPTIONS

Before we go into specific superstitious "cures," let us look at the various characteristics of magic and superstitious beliefs. These attributes become clear as a definition of either magic or superstition is attempted. Superstitions are really worn out belief systems, which means that the majority of people now no longer adhere to the original tenets. Religious beliefs become superstitions when there is a consensus of a new religious belief. So, one person's belief becomes another's superstition or magic. That makes folk belief and superstition indistinguishable from magic. All methods, regardless of their names, attempt to predict, avoid, or control certain occurrences by what has been called supernatural, or irrational, means.

The blackness of witchcraft and the occult is often hidden by the superstitious by taking the supernaturalization out of their beliefs and replacing it with the anthropomorphized, and unpredictable, Lady Luck.

Luck is not the same as chance. Chance presents us with possibilities and probabilities, with opportunities and alternatives. And it is luck, the flukes of fate, that effects our choices about these chances. Luck, however, which we can sometimes control, or try to, guides us through the chances that life presents us. The reasonable person will attempt to arrange his life in such a way that luck plays a small part. The superstitious person trusts in Lady Luck. However, she has been found to be whimsical, unpredictable and irrational. Yet, the optimists still attempt to develop more and more magical ways to get control of her. These techniques of superstition almost invariably take one of three basic forms.

One, the *omens.* Omens are the signs of the future that indicate that if such-and-such happens then this-and-that is surely and automatically to happen. This is a totally predetermined, fatalistic belief.

Examples are, "Walking under a ladder will automatically cause bad luck," and "An itchy nose brings a visitor and an itchy ear brings on a misfortune." Finding money on the ground is an omen of good luck.

Two, the *taboos*. Taboos dictate, "Do not say or do certain things or otherwise disaster will befall you or your loved ones." In primitive cultures, taboos forbade particular acts that were believed would provoke evil spirits. Today, we do not speak of evoking evil spirits, but imply their presence by considering ill fortune when and if we walk under a ladder or step on a crack.

Omens and taboos can sometimes be counteracted with swift and positive magical action. These techniques are acts of fighting magic with magic and are quite unreliable. But, surprisingly, even the superstitious are not very surprised when they fail.

Three, the *rituals*. These are actions that we should do, or could do, to bring about desired outcomes in our lives or to chase away bad luck. Crossing our fingers to bring good luck (forming a cross, of course, chases away the devils,) making a wish on birthday-cake candles or on the first star of the evening are forms of positive rituals.

The rituals can be broken down into three subcategories for simplicity.

"Imitative" magic is practiced when paintings and drawings of desired outcomes are used in rituals to attract or dispel certain things.

"Contagious" magic is the art of spell casting. The magic occurs when a person becomes ill or has bad luck after learning that a spell was cast on him.

"Sympathetic" magic is what anthropologists call a belief that whatever happens to part of something can cause it to happen to all of that something. Sticking pins in dolls or cutting parts of clothing, etc., are examples.

SPELLS AND "CURES"

Whether salt, gold, iron, rocks, fire, amulets or talismans are used, many superstitious spells and "cures" have surrounded Friday the 13th.

If you want to break the spell of Friday the 13th, go to the top of the highest mountain or building and burn all of your socks with holes in them, according to the 1987 *Old Farmers's Almanac*. If you find that that does not ward off the evil spirits, you may discover that the smell has chased away your competitors, friends and business associates.

If that is not enough, you may want to try some of the following:

Sleep with a mirror under your pillow for three Friday nights in a row. Then, on the third Friday (being Friday the 13th) you will dream of your true love and that will help oust the ill effects of Friday the 13th.

Stand on your head and chew a piece of beef gristle, then swallow it. This will break the questionable spell of Friday the 13th.

Walk around your house 13 times. According to 15th century sorcerers, this really does make you safe all day by chasing evil spirits away on Friday the 13th.

Drink a mixture of horse chestnut and skullcap herbs. This old folk charm has been suggested to make any Friday a better day, and particularly Friday the 13th.

Hang a bag of John the Conqueror root powder or grains of paradise around your neck to bring you good luck, says a sorcerer of old.

If you are prone to throwing fits, tie a sack of peony seeds around your neck. This will calm down the fits and at least make them manageable according to European magick (the old English spelling of the word.)

For those of you who are fearful of drowning or getting wet on Friday the 13th, Aristotle recommended eating garlic as a cure for hydrophobia.

Hang your shoes out of the window. This, according to a 1696 folklore prescription, will keep the sinister beings from doing you harm on this day.

Walk around the block with your mouth full of water. If you do not swallow it, you will be totally safe during Friday the 13th.

Stop trying. Quit attempting to use magic to break the harmful, magical spells of Friday the 13th. As one psychologist puts it, "Learn to be flexible. You have to give up the notion of breaking the superstitious spells of the disproved past."

But, if you must, be sure to knock on wood three times, carry the powder of an dried owl's heart with you at all times, rub your lucky rabbit's foot, sprinkle a little salt over your shoulder and remember that after this Friday the 13th, there will be only a few more Friday the 13ths until the year 2001!

Break a leg!

CHAPTER V

EASTER -

WHY THE RABBIT AND NOT THE CHICKEN?

HAVE YOU EVER WONDERED...

... why Easter has a floating date that falls on a different day each year?

... where the word "Easter" came from?

... what the ancient pre-Christian origins are of the customs of celebrating the Easter sunrise, and of lighting candles and fires?

... why some people explode fireworks on Easter day?

... when the egg first became part of the Easter celebration?

... why we color, play with and eat eggs on Easter, yet throw them on Halloween?

... how hot cross buns became part of the Easter celebration?

... what pretzels are doing in Easter history?

... if bell ringing on Easter had ancient pre-Christian origins?

... why the lily was selected as the flower of choice at Easter when it is neither a spring flower nor an American flower at all?

... why it is more customary to bathe and wear new clothes on Easter than on any other holiday of the year?

... if eating the fat from a rabbit's liver is as good as folklore says it is for curing sexual problems?

As church bells ring and choirs sing the traditional "Alleluia!", Easter services commemorate the most central belief of the Christian faith: the Resurrection of Jesus Christ. Both sacred and secular tradition surround this most celebrated of holidays.

Easter symbols are familiar to all of us, such as decorated eggs, Easter lilies, bunny rabbits, lambs, and new clothes. The customs may differ a little from country to country, but the meanings are the same. Each one has a story that goes back in history. Just like the angels and mistletoe of Christmas or the witches and jack-o-lanterns of Halloween, many have pre-Christian origins.

In 325 A.D., the Council of Nicea determined, under the chair of Emperor Constantine, that Easter should always be observed on the first Sunday that followed the first full moon on or after the vernal (spring) equinox. The spring equinox occurs around March 20. That leaves the earliest date for Easter as March 22 and the latest as April 25. Hatch, in *The American Book of Days*, says that even though Easter is a "movable" feast, Western Christians do not consider the date of the Jewish feast of freedom, Passover, to be a factor in determining the date on which it falls. However, scholars generally agree that there is more than a chronological link between the two feasts. In fact Easter is often referred to as "the Christian Passover."

HOW DID EASTER GET ITS NAME?

Be that as it may, the name for Easter in many languages, though not English or German, came from *Pesach*, the old Hebrew word for Passover. In Spanish it is *pascua;* in Greek, *Pascha*; in French, *Paques*.

Many historians believe that the name "Easter" came down to us from the ancient Norsemen. Their words *Eostur, Eastar* and *Ostar* meant "season of the growing sun" and "season of new birth," thus giving the celebration its connection with the sun.

The great eighth century English scholar Bede suggests that a Teutonic goddess of dawn and springtime named *Eostre* or *Eastre*, whose symbol was the hare, was worshiped by the Anglo-Saxon people during pre-Christian times. This, also, may be the source of our word "Easter." No one knows for sure. However, according to Edna Barth in her book *Lilies, Rabbits, and Painted Eggs: The Story of the Easter Symbols*, Easter, "definitely refers to the East and the rising sun."

WHAT IS THE ORIGIN OF THE SUNRISE WORSHIP, EASTER FIRES AND CANDLES?

"Long before there was a Christian religion, or an Easter festival, man greeted spring with joyful celebrations," says Barth. During the winter the days grew short when the sun stayed in the sky for a more brief period of time. People worried whether the sun might slip down behind a hilltop and never rise again.

At the time of the spring equinox, when the days began to be more extended and the sun shown a little longer, the people were relieved. They had hope. Life would renew itself again and crops, animals and man would thrive. Life would be rejuvenated and would be prolonged.

Scholars say the people of long ago worshiped the spirit behind the sun who sent shining life-giving rays over the fields of grain. The sun became the symbol of the resurrection.

Happy, joyful spring festivals were held for their gods. The ancient people, the Druids and others, would gather around blazing bonfires, chant and sing, dance and leap through the flames.

These ancient spring fire rites honoring the sun and performed by the pagans, as the non-Christians were called, were banned by the Christian church until the year 752 A.D. Barth says that it was then that our old Scottish friend, St. Patrick, while performing his work as a missionary revivalist, saw that the early Irish Celts and Scandinavians held spring fire rites, and were not willing to give them up.

In order to replace their "old" pagan custom, Patrick created a "new" Christian fire rite. Borrowing from the old Druidic customs, on Easter Eve he gave them huge bonfires just outside the churches. Europeans soon picked up the practice of annually blessing a new fire and it eventually became a part of the Easter Service. The custom of taking home a stick lighted from the sacred Easter fire to start the new year with a fresh start was also an old Druidic custom and shadowed the similar practices of burning the "Yule Log" at Christmas and the fire rites of Halloween.

The singular Easter candle represents the same message as Easter sunrise or Easter fire. It means that after the darkness of winter comes hope in the life of spring. After death comes life.

FIRECRACKERS ON EASTER?

Exploding fireworks of beautiful colors and shapes help celebrate the Easter festivities in many countries. You will find fireworks on Easter in Italy, Spain, Portugal and the Latin American countries. Wherever firecrackers are set off at Easter, their meanings are two-fold.

One, just like the practice of our ancient Druidic ancestors, the noise of the fireworks is intended to frighten away any evil spirits, witches or ghosts that may be near. And, two, the dazzling light and joyous explosions, just like the Easter sunrise and fires and candles that resemble the sun, symbolize that hope that life and light triumph over death and darkness.

The New Year's Eve noisemaking and the fireworks celebrations of the Fourth of July also are celebrations of freedom and independence from evil. In addition, the battles fought are represented in the explosive noises and lights on July 4th, symbolizing freedom over the darkness of tyranny.

The joyful ringing of bells during Easter week, and on Easter Sunday, is often all that remains of the noisier, more lively celebrations of earlier times. But, say the historians, the ancient, pre-Christian purpose is the same. It announces the new life of spring in happy celebrations and frightens away the spirits of darkness and evil. (See Chapter I and the ringing of bells on New Year's Day)

WHAT IS THE TRUE MEANING OF THE EASTER EGG?

The meaning of the Easter egg goes back far beyond any one religion and belongs to all of humankind. According to religious scholars and Barth, the ancient Egyptians, Persians, Phoenicians, Hindus and others believed that the world was created from an enormous egg. Then, says the Hindu myth, the World Egg broke in two, from which all else was created.

No one knows for sure whether or not this concept of the ancients started the use of Easter eggs. The majority of scholars seem to believe that eggs, like flowers, are associated with Easter as fertility symbols, reflecting ancient spring renewal rites and beliefs that have been absorbed into the paschal traditions.

Nor do we know when the painting of eggs began, but it is thought to belong to the aged practice of divination and control of the gods. Venetia Newall in volume 28 of *Man, Myth and Magic* suggests that by painting the eggs (perhaps also like the painting of faces in many primitive cultures), the evil spirits who brought bad luck would be persuaded to stay away, and the kind and moral spirits, who were the carriers of good luck, would be induced to come closer and help out. She discusses their significance, also, as symbols of life and fertility.

Only recently did Europeans drop the folk belief that the yolk of an egg laid on Good Friday, and kept for one hundred years, would turn into a diamond.

HOW DID THE HEBREW LAMB BECOME CHRISTIAN?

The Hebrew people who were among the early Christians brought with them the Passover traditional festival. Barth and other scholars say that the Jews sprinkled the blood of a lamb on their doorframes to let the angel of death know it should pass over their homes. Then the lamb had to be eaten. This Hebrew custom of the sacrificial lamb blended with the Christian customs and its meaning changed. To the

Christians, Jesus became the sacrifice. The Easter lamb became the symbol of Jesus. He is also known as the shepherd as well as the lamb. The metaphor worked well for the early pastoral peoples.

Shepherds gave secular meaning to the lamb, seeing it as an omen as well as using it for divinations and predicting the future. They believed that it was good luck to meet a lamb, especially during Easter season. According to Barth, it was considered even better luck if you saw a lamb from your window on Easter Sunday, and better luck still if the lamb was facing you. Barth indicated that the reason given was that the devil could take on any form (like the witches of Halloween) except that of a dove or a lamb.

WHAT WERE THE EARLY EASTER ANIMALS?

Through the centuries, many creatures have been considered Easter symbols. Because of their connections with Biblical, mythological or nature stories concerning renewed life, the whale, the lion and the butterfly, respectively, would be most prominent.

In the earliest of times, the bird kingdom was also represented. The renewal of its feathers by the beautiful peacock and the rising from the ashes of the mythological Phoenix were like the sun which rose every dawn bringing new hope.

WHY THE RABBIT AND NOT THE CHICKEN?

In folklore belief, the rabbit and the hare had a magical connection with witchcraft. Among their many attributed powers, witches were known for their ability to change themselves into rabbits. That is why fishermen and sailors, from ancient times, have thought of the rabbit as an ill-omen. Of course, I would too if I saw one pop up while fishing in the middle of the ocean.

But, at the same time, the rabbit has become associated with spring and especially Easter. Its presence in our secular Easter celebrations has been, according to Douglas Hill in *Magic and Superstition*, linked to its incredible reproductive abilities. This undeniable fruitfulness has made it an obvious fertility symbol.

Take one step beyond that, with the help of folklore magic, and it is easy to see why the poor rabbit, or a part of one, the foot for example, could become the magic charm to bestow fertility. The power of the rabbit's foot, historically, has been attributed to increased sexual potency and financial prosperity.

Feet, themselves, according to Sigmund Freud, have a symbolic association with sex. The lowly rabbit's foot eventually became popularized in folk belief as a symbol of general good luck. Millions of people throughout the world are comforted and reassured by carrying, and rubbing, their "lucky rabbit's foot." Perhaps people feel consoled by being thankful that they are not the rabbit!

Why does a rabbit bring Easter eggs, like Santa Claus, at Christmas, brings gifts? No one knows for sure. Hatch suggests that it appears that it happened over time by mere association of the egg and the rabbit being fertility symbols at Easter time.

THE PRETZEL AT EASTER?

The custom of eating hot cross buns on Easter, many scholars believe, grew out of the early pre-Christian, Anglo-saxon practice of honoring *Eostre*, their goddess of springtime, with wheat cakes. In an attempt to influence the new believers to abandon their pagan customs and deities, the church replaced the wheat cakes with hot cross buns. The cross of Jesus on the top was not unfamiliar to them. As an ancient pagan symbol, it was used by our ancestors to ward off evil spirits and ensure good luck. The Roman goddess of the moon and hunt, Diana, had the same configuration on her sacred cakes.

Before the early monks in England, who are known to have baked the hot cross buns, were the monks at the Vatican in Rome who made pretzels in the fifth century. They were given to the poor during Lent, the forty days before Easter. The pretzels were a symbol of Lent, just like today's hot cross buns.

Why pretzels? Look carefully at one. The monks originally intended you to see the shape of a person praying with his arms folded across his chest.

THE COLORS HAVE SYMBOLIC MEANINGS TOO?

According to Venetia Newall in *Man, Myth and Magic*, Easter is the holiday with the most symbols from the pre-Christian era, including its colors.

The white stands for purity. The yellow, the color for April, stands for sunlight and radiance. Also, Easter most frequently falls in April. Light and radiance are symbols of earthly and divine kings. The light shining from a golden sun, the apparent brightness we attribute to highly gifted people, and the "lighting up of a room" by happy and joyful people do not belong solely to Easter. Purple is also a royal color. Religiously, purple stands for mourning. But purple, Barth says, is also the color of the kings and nobility. It seems that the ancient purple dye was so expensive that only the prosperous, like the ruling class, could afford it.

WHAT? THE EASTER LILY IS NOT A SPRING FLOWER?

Thanks to the science of horticulture, we may now enjoy this fragrant, waxy lily bloom in the springtime. It is a Japanese flower that made its way to America via Bermuda. So, it is not even originally American. Like all flowers that emerge from bulbs, Barth says the lily is a symbol of life after death. But, whether the Easter plant is a lily, a tulip, a daffodil, a narcissus or the smallest dandelion in the field, all flowers, and anything green, stand for new life and new hope.

The pre-Christian Druids believed trees and plants had magical powers in them that turned them green at springtime. (See the mistletoe of Christmas) Touching a green leaf at springtime was believed to bring good health and good luck.

Barth writes that our ancient forerunners believed that "Gently switching another person with a green branch was a way of wishing him good luck." It has been called the "rod of life" and the "stroke of health." In the Chapter on St. Valentine's Day, it was also mentioned that a young girl or maiden, when tapped with the rod, was expected to become a strong and healthy adult, blessed with many children.

Remember the legendary festival honoring the Roman goddess, *Faunus*, the god of the crops, in the chapter on St. Valentine's Day? The act of lashing the young girls and women for the purpose of "purification" has been going on for centuries. The Roman soldiers, in the first century before Christ, took the custom of whipping to all parts of the world. Switching still is practiced in parts of Europe where men and boys switch the women and girls with a pussy willow.

WATER AT EASTER IS FOR DRENCHING?

Water is not as noticeable an Easter symbol as eggs and rabbits, but "drenching" or "dousing" is an ancient pagan, pre-Christian custom that is very important in Easter symbolism. Water was believed to have magical powers, and it was thought that being splashed by the newly thawed water of spring would bring good luck and good health. Maybe it had something to do with the recently discovered negative ions associated with water. Who knows?

Anyway, in another attempt to eliminate old pagan customs, and recognizing the strength of this belief, the Christian priests started the practice of blessing the ponds and streams during Easter. It was not long until people forgot the ancient beginnings of the belief in the special power of water and began to save water blessed on Easter because it had healing powers.

Although centuries have passed since it became an Easter custom, "dousing" or "drenching" is still practiced in parts of Europe today. Girls believe that to be splashed by dew, which also holds legendary powers, will make them beautiful. Boys enjoy dousing the girls and, at the end of the day, they will splash a bit on the farmer's wife so that she will give them a treat. The present-day custom of the more cosmopolitan is to spray a little perfume on one another and wish each other good luck for the coming year.

EASTER PARADES ONCE RELIGIOUS?

Off comes the old and on goes the new! Just like other Easter symbols and customs, the putting on of new clothes and parading on Easter to display them with pride, has an old, long forgotten, deep religious meaning.

Early Christians went on a special walk after church. They prayed and sang hymns at various spots along the way. A lighted candle was carried by the one at the head of the procession.

Over time, the walks became more secular, but people still dressed up in new clothes, as they do today. Even the poorest, it is believed, should wear something new, even if it is only a ribbon or a shoestring. If a young man gives a girl a pair of gloves on St. Valentine's Day, and the girl wears them on Easter Sunday, it means that she likes him, too. The custom can also be used to announce their engagement.

Even for the non-religious, Easter, with its beautiful symbols, represents the same thing to all. After darkness, there is new hope of the dawn; the constant renewal of life, love and happiness keeps us joyful that we are alive.

WANT SOME EASTER FOLKLORE OMENS, RITUALS AND REMEDIES?

To bring good luck, watch the rising sun on Easter.

For a magical charm to save the house, during Easter week cool the log of the new fire and put it away until thunder and lightning threaten the home. Then use it.

Look at a lamb on Easter Sunday to have good health and good luck.

For good luck, take a walk on Easter Sunday.

EGGS

Give your friends an egg on Easter. It will bring them good luck.

Paint it and it will bring even better luck.

Like diamonds? Take an egg laid on Good Friday, keep it for a hundred years and it will turn into one.

Feed your chickens on Holy Thursday and you will have eggs all year long.

Every egg will hatch if you set the hen on Good Friday.

To keep your food fresh longer, prepare it with eggs laid on Good Friday.

HOT CROSS BUNS

Dried hot cross buns are good for medicine.

Hardened hot cross buns are excellent charms to protect your house from lightning.

If you have rats in your cornfield, use dried hot cross buns to keep them out. (It did not say whether you should throw the hot cross buns at the rats or let the rats eat them.)

To keep your sailing vessel safe from shipwreck, carry a hardened hot cross bun with you.

FOODS

If you do not want to turn into a donkey, eat your green salad on Easter Sunday.

To ward off bad luck, eat all of your green vegetables on Easter Sunday. (Tell President Bush that that includes broccoli.)

To prevent, or cure, lice, fever, hernias and the itch, eat something green on the Thursday before Easter.

For good luck, rub yourself with a green leafy tree branch.

If you have rheumatism, the knuckles from a sheep's bone will take care of it for you.

SWITCHING

Switch a friend. To help another have good luck, lash him or her with a green branch.

Use a switch on young girls and women on Easter Sunday to assist them in having goodluck, good health and many babies.

WATER

Splash water on your friends and loved ones. This will make them healthy and strong.

For beautification, gather enough dew on Easter Sunday with which to wash your face.

Sprinkle your animals with water drawn from a spring during the Easter season. This will make them fertile and strong.

Take a bath in an icy stream and wear something new for the Easter Parade.

GOOD FRIDAY

Roosters always crow at three o'clock in the afternoon on Good Friday.

Plant radishes, lettuce, and tomatoes on Good Friday to ensure good crops.

Never dig in the ground to plant flowers on Good Friday, for you will see blood before nightfall if you do.

Plant hanging things on Good Friday. It is the chosen day for planting everything thing that hangs down, especially beans, grapes and stringing things, because Friday is "hangman's day."

Plant parsley on Good Friday and it will not go to seed.

Cabbage should be planted on Good Friday for best results.

Whooping-cough will be cured if you put the nude child in the wheat on Good Friday, and then put that wheat in the mill on the very same day. Also good for preventing that child from getting the whooping-cough.

If you have warts, get up in the morning on Good Friday and get a potato. Don't speak to anyone. Go to the barn, cut the potato in two, rub it over the wart and then feed the potato to the cow. The warts will go away.

Have a rupture? Then get a soft-shelled egg that was laid on Good Friday, take the skin off the egg and put it over the rupture. Name the three greatest names (Father, Son, and Holy Ghost) and the rupture will go away.

Go fishing on Good Friday, for fish always bite on that day.

RABBITS

It is considered a good omen if a rabbit crosses your path in front of you. It is bad luck, however, if it crosses behind you.

The milk of a hare will cure whooping cough.

Eating the fat from a rabbit's liver will cure sexual problems and give you sexual prowess.

Rubbing a rabbit's foot will bring you good luck. For even better luck, procure the left, hind one. The luck-bearing properties will increase even more if the rabbit is sacrificed at the full of the moon, in a cemetery, by a red-haired, cross-eyed woman.

Easter is a great religious holiday venerating the resurrection our Lord Jesus Christ. Along with the joy of the deep religious meaning, the fun of the lighthearted secular customs can, as well, be experienced. We don't have to give up either to pray for the ending of darkness in this world and celebrate the hope of a brighter future and blessings of a better place for all humankind.

CHAPTER VI

APRIL FOOLS' DAY -

ORIGINS, PRANKS, PHOBIAS AND "CURES"

HAVE YOU EVER WONDERED...

... when the custom of pulling pranks and tricks on friends and relatives began?

... why was, and is, the victim considered the fool?

... if we pull pranks as an echo of some ancient fertility rites?

... what "hunting the *gowk*" or "April fish" have to do with April fooling?

... how the practices of fools' errands and April Fools' jokes got to the United States and Canada?

... why, in some countries, this day is called "All Fools' Day?

... what some of the common, and not so common, childhood April Fools' Day pranks are?

... what types of jokes and April foolings are indulged in by adults?

... what some common phobias are surrounding April Fools' Day?

... if we should stop celebrating April Fools' Day because people are often offended or say that jokes are harmful?

> **... what the best remedy is for overcoming anxieties and warding off evil spirits on the day of fools' errands and pranks?**

SOURCES OF APRIL FOOLS' DAY

April Fools' Day or All Fool's Day, is the holiday day of freedom for the prankster.

It is striking that at this time of year, although not always precisely on April 1, customs of fooling people are found in lands as far apart as Sweden, Portugal and India. Whatever its ancient origins, the celebration of the day came into common practice as early as 1582 in France and in the 18th century in England.

On this day, practical jokes may be guiltlessly played with freedom, such as sending people on foolish errands or putting salt in the sugar bowl. According to *Funk & Wagnalls Standard Dictionary of Folklore, Mythology and Legend*, the practice is found in both a Scottish custom, which is called *hunting the gowk, cuckoo or fool* (the source of our word "cuckoo" meaning crazy or silly,) and *Poisson d'avrir* (the fish of April) in France. In England, the terms April *gob, gawby, or gobby* are used.

The claims of the origins of April Fools' Day are varied. Often the theories are found to be as creative and whimsical as the April Fools' jokes themselves.

One of these theories involves the unsuccessful journey of the dove who was sent from the ark by Noah to survey the contryside. Another is the variable weather during that season.

Other historians believe that both the French and Scottish customs of pulling pranks possibly reflect the general feelings of the ancient spring sexual license, as well as an antiquated echo of the Druidic priests' efforts to deceive evil spirits which might, as was believed, interfere with fertility during the planting, sprouting and mating season.

Cohen and Coffin the editors of *The Folklore of American Holidays*, say that the custom of April fooling is also associated with civil and church rebellion such as the Lord of Misrule's ceremonies. As his name suggests, he was the director of wild, unruly feasts and masquerades with people dressed as exotic animals or mythological beasts.

Even though the ancient historical origin of the custom is vague and uncertain, scholars seem to lean toward it having come about in France as a result of the change from the Julian calendar to the Gregorian calendar in 1582. It was then that the New Year was moved from March 25 to January 1. Thus, the first "April fools" may have been the inflexible people who were unable, or unwilling to make the "proper" adjustment.

Many different explanations have been offered for the origins of April Fools' Day. As Jane Hatch, the editor of *The American Book of Days* states, in 1760 the confusion was set to verse in *Poor Robin's Almanac:*

> *"The first of April, some do say,*
> *Is set apart for All Fools' Day.*
> *But why the people call it so,*
> *Nor I, nor they themselves do know.*
> *But on this day are people sent*
> *On purpose for pure merriment."*

ROMAN SOURCE

Another early, and highly debatable theory, is that April Fools' Day is a relic of the festival of *Cerealia,* held at the beginning of April in Roman times. Hatch goes on to say that "this festival recalled the legend in which the goddess Ceres hears the echo of Proserpina, her daughter, screaming as she is being carried off to the lower world from the Elysian meadows by Pluto. Ceres then goes in search of Proserpina's voice. But Ceres' search is a fool's errand, for it is impossible to find the echo."

April was originally the second month in the ancient Roman year, when the calendar began with March. The origin of its name is still being debated by scholars. The most commonly accepted theory, Hatch says, is that "Aprilis," the Roman name for the month, is derived from the Latin verb *aperire,* meaning "to open" (referring to the fertile blossoming of buds on trees and flowers in this time and the mating season).

Most scholars think that the month *April* was first called *Aphrilis,* a Latin name coming from *Aphrodite*, the Greek goddess of love like the Roman goddess of love, *Venus*. Because April was sacred to her, the first day of the month was chosen for her festival.

CELTIC DRUIDS SOURCE

Some believe that April Fools' Day is a vestige of an early spring Celtic custom. As was mentioned earlier, this custom was believed to possibly reflect the feelings of spring sexual license that many feel, aside from other folklore such as New Year's Day and St. Valentine's Day.

Some of the fertility practices of the Druidic priests were efforts to deceive evil spirits which might interfere with fertility at the time when planting, sprouting and mating are occurring. According to D. J. Conway, in his book *Celtic Magic,* by pulling pranks, the ill-doers and spirits, would become confused and the rituals would be more successful.

SPRING EQUINOX SOURCE

Hatch says, that "The impression prevails, however, that the custom of April fooling had something to do with the observance of the spring equinox (usually March 21 in the Gregorian calendar)."

In the folklore of some European countries, she goes on to say, at least part of the connection may be that, at the vernal equinox, "nature seems to play with human beings, sending them sunshine or rain according to whim," as well as playing with their hearts and stimulating the mating instincts. (See also St. Valentine's Day in Chapter II)

INDIA HINDU FESTIVAL OF HOLI THEORY

Unbelievable as it may seem, and definitely fascinating to scholars, is the similarity of the European April fooling to one aspect of the Hindu festival of Holi (or Huli). Holi, also, was originally an ancient fertility rite held at the beginning of spring.

This fire festival, which lasts for five days, includes outdoor bonfires and dancing which sends the people into high spirits. The surprising common thread between Holi and the European April Fools' Day is that on March 31, the last day of the festival, people are sent on witless errands, much to the amusement of all concerned. This common thread may indicate their mutual origin in an even more ancient custom.

However, Jane Hatch suggests that "it seems just as likely ... that the European and Hindu celebrations arose quite separately, and in different eras, to incarnate a common human fascination with themes of imposture and gullibility, wisdom and foolishness, and 'loss of face.'"

On the other hand, Celtic historians Isabel Elder and Merch Derri suggest that in 1800 B.C. the Druids in Northern Europe were influenced by invaders from the Orient, suggesting that this could be the connection and the reason its practice seems so universal.

Even though the folk tales of many peoples have fool's errands included, the fact still does not answer the question as to why these customs often take place at the beginning of spring. I believe it has to do with the mating season and why reasonable people go "crazy" and conduct themselves with silly and erratic behavior when they fall in love. (See Chapter II on St. Valentines Day and pheromones).

Be as it may, love, romantic craziness, silliness and fooling around surround this season.

THE GREGORIAN CALENDAR AND APRIL FOOLS' DAY

With all its similarities, April Fools' Day came to the American Colonies with the English, Scottish and possibly the French settlers.

The first mention of the day in England occurred in England in Dawks's Newsletter of April 2, 1698, but must have been practiced long before that.

France may have been the neighbor who influenced the English to participate in the foolery, because its calendar was changed in 1564 by Charles IX, thus changing New Year's from March 25 to January 1. However, there were many "fools" who continued to observe the old New Year.

Rome had already been observing this practice long before the time of Christ.

Charles IX's proclamation took years to be recognized because of the difficulty in changing old habits and the slow methods of communication in his time.

The biggest objection to change came from the Conservatives. After a while, the liberals began to ridiculing the die-hards for hanging on to the old New Year's custom. They would invent reasons to make phony calls and send the die-hards mock gifts on April 1. It is thought that the popular French tradition of April fooling came from practices like these.

No one knows why, in France, the hoax is an "April fish," a *Poisson d'avril*. Maybe it is because the best fishing is in April, or because the sun, under the Julian calendar, was leaving the zodiacal sign of Pisces (the Fish). Whatever the reason, in France today confectioners display chocolate fish in their windows on April 1, and friends send each other anonymous postcards with pictures of fish.

In England and the British colonies, March 25 remained the New Year until 1751-1752; in Scotland, until 1600. Regardless of whether April fooling came to the British Isles from France or originated from the celebrations on April 1 as the last day of the New Year's festival, the custom of playing jokes on others on April 1st has been built up in practically all of the English-speaking world.

MEXICO AND OTHER COUNTRIES

December 28 is All Fool's Day in Mexico. Anyone naive enough to lend an item on that day is the "fool," because custom dictates that it need not be returned. He may expect, instead, a box of candies or other small objects with a message reminding him that he has been fooled.

The day is also popular in Italy, Spain, Portugal, Sweden, Germany and Norway. In the latter two, it is celebrated on the first and last days of April.

APRIL FOOL PRANKS AND JOKES

As we all know, the goal of April fooling has always been to successfully pull some prank on another who has not yet noticed what day it is. When the victim realizes that he has been tricked, the trickster calls out "April fool!"

The most popular form of April fooling has customarily been the "fool's errand," according to Hatch "in which an unsuspecting person is sent on an absurd mission--for example, to buy some pigeon's milk, a copy of the *History of Adam's Grandfather*" or a sky-hook on which to hang something.

The French delight in sending the unwary fool on an errand for sweet vinegar. Of course, everyone he asks is instantly aware of the joke. "Thus by contrivers' inadvertent jest, One fool exposed makes pastime for the rest," runs an old rhyme.

Hatch quotes the century old writing of the antiquarian Robert Chambers as saying, "'For successful April fooling, it is necessary to have some considerable degree of coolness and face, One of the charms of the day is the chance it gives to try out the poker face.'"

It is important to do your April fooling before noon because the slow prankster is traditionally called the "April fool" for attempting his trickery too late in the day.

Outside the home, the custom of playing pranks is generally celebrated by schoolchildren. The fooling includes nonsensical errands, trick candy, fake spilled milk and the ever popular pocketbook on a string to yank away from the unsuspecting finder. They may pin a sign that says "kick me" on a friend's back, snickering to themselves as they wait for his discovery.

The ever popular "brick under the hat" trick brings great delight as pranksters wait for someone to kick it out of his way. Chocolate covered candies stuffed with cotton, or salt and pepper, may also be deviously served.

Seriously informing an adult that there is a hole in his sweater, a spot on her blouse, or mud on his face brings great delight to some children.

April Fools' Day joking and fooling have persisted in American folk ways and practices since Colonial times. Even though the jokes have naturally not received official recognition or encouragement from schools or the Federal government, they are, however, more than occasionally mentioned in print and discussed on radio and television. In fact, the author has been interviewed in newspapers and magazines, on TV and the radio, for over 40 years discussing this day. April Fool! It's been only one year.

Why has April Fools' Day persisted? Authorities have suggested that perhaps one reason is that children (as with most holidays of fun) are often introduced to it within their own family unit. They either have jokes played on them or see their parents playing a joke on each other. These provide the rare opportunity for children to see the "child" in their parents and to laugh together.

MORE APRIL FOOLS' TRICKS

The following pranks and tricks, for the most part, are found in *The American Book of Days* or *The Folklore of American Holidays*.

A teacher in 1864 would trick her class on April 1 with, "Oh, come out and see the flock of wild geese!"

Children would trick each other by yelling, "Oh, look at that little bird," "It's snowing," "You have a black mark on your face," etc. Tying a rag on the back of the teacher's dress or pinning a label on the back that reads "kick me!" were popular when I was growing up.

Other reliable pranks were filling the sugar bowl with salt, stuffing a biscuit with paper and offering an empty egg shell at breakfast.

Gluing a coin to the pavement, stuffing an old purse with paper and dropping it; tying handkerchiefs to strings, dropping them, then pulling them back when almost picked up by an unwitting passerby were favorite performances.

Today, as in the past, these pranks and jokes are still being played.

A common prank is to make up any kind of story such as "Your shoe is untied," and when the person looks, say, "April Fool." If it is the day after April 1, he should say,

"Ha, ha. April Fool's gone and past;

You're the biggest fool at last."

Other forms of mischief include:

Putting dirt-filled coffee sacks in the road and waiting to see who picks them up.

Setting fire to a manure-filled paper bag, then watching the person's face turn to surprised disgust as he stamps out the fire.

APRIL FOOL BY ADULTS

Adults of all ages enjoy playing pranks, like the mother who cooked pancakes filled with cloth circles so that no one could cut them. Similarly an employee may stuff cotton or paper in the staff's croissants or donuts.

As mentioned in *The Folklore of American Holidays*, Catherine Harris Ainsworth published a number of accounts of pranks played by adult factory and office workers in the Buffalo area of New York in her book *American Calendar Customs*.

Cohen and Coffin write that "One involved bakery employees in collusion with the manager telling a girl who had just finished her shift that she was to substitute for the next shift as well." Another involved "putting red pepper in a worker's coffee thermos. He took the prank seriously and thought the boss had done it. The trick resulted in an argument. The man quit, and ultimately ran off with the boss's secretary. Such childish tricks as taping down telephone hooks so the phone will continue to ring after being answered, taping filing cabinets closed, and stapling folders together seem to have been common, as were more elaborate pranks such as faking phone calls, issuing invitations for nonexistent parties, and creating bomb scares."

Telephone jokes were common when I was growing up, as they are today. It is considered hilarious, by some, to tell a co-worker that "Mr. Fox" or "Miss Fish" called while they were out and to watch their embarrassed expression when they return the call to what turns out to be the zoo or the pet shop.

Butchers, also, receive many calls for Mrs. Lamb or Mr. Weiner on April Fools' Day.

April Fool letters have been around since antiquity. Radio jokes and April fooling have gone computerized as well, with April 1 viruses widely rumored to go off and shut down computer programs. An official notice by the University of Pennsylvania Computing Resource Center was published in the Almanac, the University's internal newsletter of March 27, 1990. This proved to be an "April Fool." The warning was widely circulated but the virus did not materialize. Unfortunately, some in 1992 did.

In recent years, according to Jane Hatch, at least two promotional events in the United States have used April Fools' Day as their starting point.

She states that "since 1945 the Humor Society of America has sponsored National Laugh Week during the first 10 days of April to honor and draw public attention to aspiring and well-known comedians--the 20th century's 'court jesters.'"

"Publicity Stunt Week has also been sponsored by a public relations firm during the first week of April since 1960 to increase commercial and popular awareness of the effectiveness of publicity stunts in bringing persons or products into the news dramatically. Unusual and intriguing stunts are encouraged and an award is given for the top stunt of the year."

APHRILOPHOBIA AND OTHER PHOBIAS

Similar to the anxieties and phobias besetting Friday the 13th, there are genuinely scary feelings that continue to surround April 1 for many. These can be seen in the fact that people, even in today's world, often hesitate to schedule or perform important acts, such as marrying or launching a new business enterprise on April 1.

Not as many people suffer from anxieties and phobias as they do around Friday the 13th or Halloween, but sufferers there are.

Phobias surrounding this day mainly fall into the category of Social phobias. People who suffer excessively from the fear of being ridiculed, losing face, blushing, being embarrassed or put-down in social situations have this type of phobia.

Some of these phobias are:

Aphrilophobia -   fear of April Fools' Day itself.

Katagelophobia -   fear of ridicule or embarrassment.

Neophobia -   fear of the novel or something new.

Scopophobia -   fear of being stared at.

Ereuthophobia -   fear of blushing.

Mythophobia -   fear of making a false statement.

Traumatophobia -   fear of being emotionally wounded or injured.

Aphrilis is a Latin name derived from Aphrodite, the Greek goddess of love whom the Romans equated with Venus, and is believed to have eventually become "April."

Symptoms range from mild, almost unnoticed anxiety to full blown panic attacks where people will not even go to work for fear of having a joke or prank pulled on them. Some people have reported being almost petrified worrying about what someone might do at work on this day.

I once had a patient, a 32 year old accountant, who would not leave her house on April Fools' Day.

On this day, especially, the talk show hosts have a fear called "no-guest-a-phobia," the fear of having their guests cancel out at the last minute.

Thus the day's traditional association with duplicity has its effects. Some are able to ignore this, however, and some are not. According to *The American Book of Days*, the most famous case of blatantly and intentionally defying the spirits was Napoleon I of France, who married his second wife, Marie-Louise of Austria, on April 1, 1810. For this his subjects called him the "April fish."

Some people have voiced their concern about prank pulling and April fooling as childish and unnecessary acts of pre-pubescent foolishness. They sometimes go on to say that it is a waste of time and can often be harmful to the recipients of the jokes.

I happen to see it the other way around. I believe that if you stay away from pranks that are obviously physically or mentally harmful to someone and stick with the harmless ones (like stuffing donuts with paper for a laugh) you will be displaying healthy emotional behavior.

Mentally healthy people have a sense of humor and can give and take a good joke. In my book, *Keying: The Power of Positive Feelings*, I devote an entire chapter on the power of smiling, laughing, having a good time and being happy. In fact, beneficial hormones are released when you are happy and having a good time, including pulling a joke on someone or having them do it to you. That increases your physical health and life span. Deepak Chopra, the famous endocrinologist, in his many books mentions *interlukins* and *interferons* as some of the positive chemicals that are released into the body when one is feeling good and is perceiving the world as a fun place in which to live.

Also, linguistically and psychologically, when people pull tricks on each other, it is really a statement of their caring for each other. It is a sociably acceptable and healthy way to interact with another and to let people in your life know that they mean something to you. If you search your heart and find that that is not true, then I would suggest that you not pull the trick on that person because it could be expressing anger, hostility or resentment in disguise.

The best thing to do then would be to back off, lighten up and search your inner self as to why you find it necessary to hold on to the resentment or anger or fear (because fear will be found at the bottom line supporting your anger or hostility). You may find, as do many of my patients, that holding on is a way to hide your perceived insecurities and to make you feel stronger. Vulnerability and openness is the only way to have fun and live a truly happy, healthy and lengthy life.

The best prescription I can give for anyone on April Fools' Day, it seems, is to continue in the ancient folklore tradition, not being concerned with superstitions or ill-fate, but with the therapeutic powers of laughter and good fun.

CHAPTER VII

HALLOWEEN -

SORCERY, MYTH, FOLKLORE AND PHOBIAS

HAVE YOU EVER WONDERED...

... why October 31 was specifically chosen to be the holiday of witches, black cats, owls, Jack-O-Lanterns and goblins?

... how Halloween got its name?

... how witches became associated with Halloween?

... why today's witches are so often depicted as ugly old women with matted hair and bony fingers, rather than men?

... why most witches are seen with broomsticks rather than mops?

... how black cats and owls became linked with Halloween?

... if goblins ever really existed at some time?

... how the Jack-O-Lantern got its name?

... what the origin of wearing Halloween masks is?

... where the custom of "trick or treating" came from?

... what the clinical name for the "fear of Halloween" is?

... if people who are superstitious or believe in witchcraft are likely to be mentally ill and should seek help?

... **what the difference between superstitions, beliefs and phobias is?**

... **if some superstitions are positive?**

... **why the "Witch Hunts of Salem" have been compared to psychiatry and psychotherapy as currently being practiced?**

... **what some folklore "cures" are that surround Halloween?**

... **what some up-to-date suggestions are for handling these fears?**

Start with ancient pre-Christian rituals; add a dose of the macabre and a pinch of the poppycock. Season generously with fact and folklore. Stir vigorously, and you end up with Halloween.

Not many holidays have a more strange or ambiguous history than Halloween, which falls on October 31. For Roman Catholics, Anglicans, and Lutherans, it is the eve of the most important feast of the church year, All Saints' Day - also known as All Hallows' Day or All Hallowmass. In such countries as France, Spain, and Italy, All Hallows' Eve is observed solemnly as a serious religious event, but in the British Isles, and, especially, the United States, it is generally regarded as a night for pranksters, party-goers and fortune tellers.

Because Halloween has lost its real meaning, social scientists call it a "degenerate celebration." Tell that to the children who won't let it die!

According to *The American Book of Days*, some of the traditional customs and practices surrounding Halloween "commemorate rites and creatures that Christianity has over the centuries adamantly opposed; auguries, ghosts, witches, goblins, and fairies."

Let us take a look at Halloween's religious and secular history and see how the strange mixture has affected our present-day celebration.

WHERE AND WHEN DID HALLOWEEN BEGIN?

In its more popular or folk aspects, Halloween is a combination of ancient Druidic practices and pre-Christian Roman religious beliefs.

Over 2,000 years ago the Celtic order of priestly Druids, originating in Gaul, celebrated their year's end on Oct. 31, the eve of *Samhain* which means "summer's end." Their holiday meant the end of summer and the beginning of winter. Their New Year began on November 1.

On this occasion the priestly Druids performed their joint mystical ceremonies in honor of their great sun god, *Baal*, who helped with the newly stored grains, fruits, and nuts, and their lord of the dead, *Samhain*. The spirit behind the sun was joyfully thanked for the harvest, and rites were held for the moral support needed in the coming battle with the cold and darkness of winter.

The Celts also believed that the fate of the souls of deceased persons for the coming year was decided by the lord of the dead when he gathered their souls on October 31. These spirits were thought to have permission to visit their living relatives briefly to obtain a little warmth and comfort for the cold winter ahead. Some of the more frustrated ghosts played pranks on human beings and caused supernatural happenings. Farmers would attempt to protect their cows by hanging blessed bells around the animals' necks.

The Druidic priests had the people put out their fires at home, and, by rubbing branches of the sacred oak tree together, start "new fire." From the "new fire," big bonfires were lighted and kept burning all through the night in order to honor the sun god, scare away the "ornery" ghosts and light the way for the more kindly ones. This has a striking similarity to those fire rites practiced during Easter and for Midsummer Eve in June.

Our modern Halloween also has some elements that originated from the ancient Romans. The Romans conquered the Celts in A.D. 43 and ruled over them for more than 400 years. During this period, two autumn festivals were combined with the Celtic festival of Samhain. One was the festival honoring *Pomona*, the goddess of fruits and trees. Some scholars indicate that this celebration had a small part in determining our present-day observances of Halloween, especially in the use of fruit and nuts for fortune-telling. Apples probably became associated with Halloween because of this festival. The other celebration was called *Feralia,* which was a feast held in late October not unlike that of the Celtic tribes, to honor the dead.

The Romans, and later the Roman Church, used lies and propaganda in order to pillage the Druids' tin, gold, enamelled art and products of their rich commerce (For more on this, see Chapter III on St. Patrick's Day). The Roman Emperors, according to Edna Barth in *Witches, Pumpkins, and Grinning Ghosts: The Story of Halloween Symbols*, were also disturbed because some of the Roman soldiers were adopting "the beliefs of the Druids, and there were Druid converts in Rome itself."

The Druid religion was banned and the Druid priests were hunted and killed. But the Celts held on to their Druidic customs and, in the face of danger, they continued to prepare for the visitations of the spirits and built their Samhain bonfires.

The Christian Church, in the fourth century, was declared lawful by the Roman Emperor Constantine. Once it became the law of the Roman land, the church became frightened of being overcome by, what it considered, the overly popular paganistic rites of the Druids. Pope Gregory III, in the eight century, had the usual feast honoring all of the saints, which was held in May, moved to November. This was done, no doubt, to absorb the strongly ingrained paganism that remained from the old Samhain rites.

About a hundred years later, Pope Gregory IV decreed that All Hallows' Eve would fall on October 31 as the vigil of All Saints' Day (All Hallowmass or All Hallows' Day). All Saints' Day would fall on November 1 and All Soul's Day on November 2.

The Lord of the Dead festival of the Druids became a Christian festival of the dead. Thus, the church was able to hold on to its newly acquired "followers" by allowing the people to continue a festival they had celebrated long before becoming Christians.

The reason the church needed an All Saints' Day was because it honored many martyrs and saints, and assigned them their own day on the calendar. Eventually, the church ran out of days because there were fewer days on the calendar than there were saints to venerate. So it decided to incorporate them all into one day.

However, as hard as the church tried to discourage it,the Celtic people who later became the Scotch, Irish and English, over the centuries continued practicing, secretly, some of the older Samhain rites. Eventually, the rituals turned toward a more secular vein and Halloween has become what we know it to be today, fun and games for children and adults alike.

Thanks are due the Scottish and Irish people who, even though they were running from the great potato famine of the nineteenth century, brought Halloween to the United States and Canada. And thanks to them for bringing along with it the witches, cats, bats, devils, demons and goblins, bobbing for apples, ghosts, fortune telling, jack-o-lanterns and all the other wonderful folklore of this enchanting holiday.

HALLOWEEN MEANS WHAT?

Halloween became what it is by a series of contractions and linguistic metamorphoses. Because it was the evening of All Hallows' Day, it naturally became All Hallows' Evening. Quickly said, as the people of Brittany did, it became All Hallows' Even'. That, quickly said, became All Hallowe'en, and, being lazy, the All was eventually dropped which left Halloween.

WHY WITCHES ON HALLOWEEN?

Witches at Halloween have the strangest of all histories. For thousands of years, the Greeks, Romans, Stone Age "little people" and the Celtics believed in sorcerers, magicians, and witchcraft.

Anthropologists say that some 20 thousand years ago, these were our early "scientists." They attempted to answer questions about their world and tried to make order out of it.

It is believed by some scholars that the practices of the Stone Age "little people," who worshipped a horned god in a celebration of animal hunts and fortune telling around October, were the very beginnings of magic and witchcraft in the Western world.

The practice of their magic included the three fascinating components as defined in Chapter IV about Friday the 13th. Using *imitative magic*, they believed that by painting and drawing activities that they desired to have happen, the gods, or spirits would make them happen or duplicate them in real life. The cave paintings of twenty thousand years ago were drawn by our first "scientists."

Another was *contagious magic*. Parts of clothing, or a lock of hair or fingernails were used. It was (and is in parts of the world) believed that when the victim learned that a spell had been cast on him, he would become ill or die.

The third was *sympathetic magic. Voodoo* is one common method of this kind of magic. Sticking pins in dolls or burning someone in effigy are both examples.

Our ancient ancestors believed that magic charms, spells and predictions were very powerful on the eve of Samhain because of the many spirits roaming freely who might be induced to help. Woe be to you if you ignored them.

The sorcerer knew a lot about plants, herbs and animal parts that seemed magical. This knowledge gave him power over the people, and he wanted to keep this power a secret. The word *occult* means hidden. So the magic became the hidden knowledge, or occult, in order to protect the powers of the "scientist." Unfortunately, this practice of acting as if knowledge is supposed to be kept secret, it appears, has not changed much with some present-day religious beliefs, scientists and psychologies.

Anthropologists contend that when the magicians' sorcery failed in its fight against the strength of nature, as it often did, people helplessly began to regard those powers as gods. Then they attempted to influence the gods to fulfill human desires, but whatever happened was now the will of the gods.

Edna Barth suggests that priests come into being to interpret this "will of god." Magic was then, of course, banned, and by the 5th century, Roman law ordered anyone killed who was caught using it. The harmless magic of healing the sick or preparing love potions was accepted. Historically, after the priests, there was the arrival of the scientists, and finally the development of the present-day psychologists and psychiatrists. Each of these groups arrived on the scene to continue the work of the sorcerers. It is believed by Deepak Chopra, M.D., and others, that these contemporary "scientists" have ideas and practices that are to be considered as present-day superstitions.

However, in the Middle Ages, the echo of the Druidic beliefs that Halloween was the gathering time for unsatisfied spirits persisted. This belief found a safe harbor in the cult of witchcraft. The word *witch* comes from *wica*, the Saxon word for *wise one*.

Celebrations or festivities called Witches' Sabbaths became popular. Barth writes that it is believed that these celebrations derived from the ancient religion of the Horned God and the followers were called witches. *Covens* were groups of 13 witches gathered together to practice the rites and ceremonies of magic. The 13th was the master teacher of the coven.

There were two major Witches' Sabbaths during the year. One was on the eve of May Day, the day of mating, and the other on October 31, the day of hunting and celebration of the capture of animals. The most sacred, well known spots for these celebrations were Puyde Dome, France; Blocula, Sweden and Hartz, Germany.

Witches Sabbaths were joyful occasions with spring dances, feasts and celebration, and people looked forward to them. All this appealed to the masses in comparison to the drab religious practices of the Romans.

By the 10th century these beliefs and practices became more popular than Christianity. The prospect of being outnumbered by the extremely popular pagan cult was alarming the Church, so it branded all people practicing this paganism as evil emissaries of the Devil. And, by the Middle Ages, the Christian devil, the enemy of the church, had been assigned horns, a forked tail and cloven hooves to resemble the pagans' horned god. The metamorphosis of the appearance of the devil was intentional and used to scare and control the masses.

In the 13th Century the Witch Hunts were beginning to take place. At first it was acceptable to make love potions, but it was not permissible to predict death or bad weather. Then came the Inquisitions. They were, at first, held to exterminate the heretics, not the witches. But, in 1484, Pope Innocent VIII attacked witches, as well as heretics, as the devil's agents.

It has been estimated that nine million people were burned or hanged, according to Barth. Catholic and Protestant alike felt justified by the passage from the Bible, "Thou shalt not suffer a witch to live."

Scholars believe the true reason for the horrible witch hunts is that the Druidic religious practices, handed down from the Stone Age "little people," really could have overtaken the Roman church.

By the 19th century, few educated people anywhere took witchcraft very seriously. However, Barth indicated that both the less educated and the rural people went right on believing in witches. And over time, at Halloween the souls of the deceased that were believed to change into goblins and other beings that had always been feared, became mainly witches.

WHY ARE WITCHES SEEN MOSTLY AS UGLY WOMEN?

When we think of today's witches, we think of them, as they are so often depicted, as ugly old women with snarled hair, snaggly teeth, bony fingers and broomsticks, rather than as men. Why?

It is an historical disservice to women! First, there were many men, as well as women and children, attending the Witches' Sabbaths. The women enjoyed equality in the cult which they did not have in any other area of their lives.

Second, the Roman Church leaders were all men, and, some scholars believe, when they banned witchcraft as evil they included women in that judgment because women were considered less than human and in need of being controlled. So, during the Witch Hunts, it was men who did the judging and women did not have a very fair chance.

And third, the women witches who attended these Sabbaths, rather than the men, did most, if not all, of the cooking and were often seen stirring the big pots. Most women of the times, Barth says, also brewed cauldrons of medicinal herbs to cure the ailments of their families and friends. When the skeptics looked in at this from the outside, they erroneously concluded that the women were concocting witches' brews.

In the final analysis, women got a bum rap!

WHY BROOMSTICKS AND NOT MOPS?

It is fascinating and interesting that most of the witches seen at Halloween are using broomsticks as their favorite mode of transportation. Why broomsticks and not magic carpets?

In some of the dances during the Witches' Sabbaths, Barth tells of people who galloped about straddling branches or broomsticks. In other dances, they felt a oneness with their horned god as they moved about with rhythmic gestures. The sounds and movements gave them a sense of euphoria.

There were also Spring Jumping Dances in which the witches believed that the higher they jumped, the better the crops would grow or the more fertile they, personally, would become. The non-believers, looking in from the outside, could see nothing but people jumping as high as they could on broomsticks and concluded that witches rode broomsticks.

And, funniest of all, is the story of the assortment of people, some rich, some poor, who attended the Witches' Sabbaths. Barth tells of how the nobility and well-to-do rode on horses or in carriages drawn by horses or people, while the poorer folk had to walk. Because Halloween fell during the rainy season, those less well-off carried brooms or sticks to pole vault over the muddy puddles and creeks to keep from getting wet. Seeing this, outsiders mistakenly passed the news around that the witches were flying on broomsticks!

WHY ARE BLACK CATS AND OWLS HARBINGERS OF EVIL?

Historically, cats have always been thought of as possessing magical powers. The first tamed cats were recorded in ancient Egypt. They were used in the great grain storehouses as protectors from rats and mice. The Egyptian *Pasht* was a cat-headed goddess.The early Greeks and Romans honored the goddess *Hecate* who ruled over witches, wizards, and ghosts. Her priestess was a woman who had been turned into a cat.

The Phoenicians kept cats on ships to keep the mice population down, and were so valuable that they were traded in Europe for tin.

In Norse mythology *Freya* was the goddess of beauty, love and marriage, and of the dead (I can not help but wonder why marriage and death were combined!) Anyway, her chariot was drawn by cats.

Cats were closely linked with the Druid *Samhain* feasts, and later with witches, and were considered the spirit of evil. The Druids dreaded cats and believed that they were once humans transformed into cats by supernatural forces. During the Samhain festivities, cats were often sacrificed in the fires to ward off bad luck in the coming year.

Later in history, the Europeans believed that witches had *familiars* which were little animals, often called *imps* if they were domesticated. These familiars took on the shape of cats especially, but could be seen as toads, bats, spiders and anything else as well. Their main job was to help the witches exercise their magical powers.

The belief in familiars was so widespread that Barth tells of a rooster in London, thought to have been a witch's familiar, that was summoned to court and tried by a group of learned judges. And, as the story goes, no one saw anything ridiculous in that at all!

Black cats seem to have been singled out, specifically, as the most common of the witches' familiars and a symbol of evil. Actually, it is believed, that the cat can be any color on Halloween. They all look black in the dark. And, since the beginning of recorded history, black has always been considered to be associated with evil and things sinister.

Halloween owls have a chameleon-like past. In ancient times, the Romans believed that the owl was the most common harbinger of evil. Greece, on the other hand, saw the owl as sacred. *Athene*, the Greek goddess of wisdom, used an owl as her familiar. In the Middle Ages, and even to this day for the superstitious, screeches and glassy stares from owls meant death and disaster. The truth of their identity? Who-o-o-o knows!

WHO ARE THE GOBLINS?

Some scholars suggest that goblins really existed in some ancient time. During the Stone Age, short, dark-skinned *little people* lived in the forests of Northern Europe and The British Isles. They were conquered, it is believed, by the invading Germanic and Celtic tribes.

These little people lived in low, dome-shaped huts that looked like mounds. They wore green clothing, probably to hide in the woods better, and the Celts thought they were *fairies* and, of course, evil spirits. The French called them g*oblins,* which means *little people* or fairy folk. Goblins were blamed for any and all kinds of misfortunes including having trouble churning cream into butter, preventing the cow from giving milk, the chickens from laying eggs and the wife from having babies.

Very little is known regarding the religious practices of the little people except that, every seven years, according to Barth, they made human sacrifices to their gods. For this ritual, they were known to steal children from the Celts. That is where the saying, "You had better watch out or the goblins will get you" came from. That, by the way, is the first systematic child-rearing practice ever recorded.

These little people were extremely afraid of the superior iron weapons of their enemies, and the loud noises of bells. Thus, both bells and horseshoes became weapons used against evil spirits and bad luck. Horseshoes were doubly frightening to the little people because they looked like the Celtic moon god's crescent.

WHAT IS THE ORIGIN OF THE JACK-O-LANTERN?

When you see grinning pumpkins bobbing up and down, carried by youngsters on Halloween night, do you wonder what curious events occurred to have caused them to be named *Jack-O-Lanterns*?

According to historians, Jack-O-Lanterns were originally carried by the Scottish children. They were made from the largest turnips they could find by carving faces on them and putting candles inside. The children called them *bogies* and carried them on Halloween to scare away the witches. This is where the term *bogeyman* comes from. The Irish used potatoes and turnips. The English preferred beets and called them *mangel-wurzels*.

Then, when Scottish and Irish children came to the new country, they saw, for the first time, big, beautiful, soft, round pumpkins growing all over. Being creative, they at once realized what perfect Jack-O'-Lanterns those pumpkins would make. And they certainly did.

Many early English people would not admit to ghosts, but, as Barth indicates, would confess to seeing Lantern Men. These Lantern Men were also called *Hob-O'-Lantern, Jack-O'-Lantern, Will-O'-the-Wisp or Will*. Often they were called Corpse Candles because they were seen as moving lights over marshes, bogs or freshly dug graves.

In areas where lights were floating above the marshes, it was believed that if one would follow one of these Will-O'-the-Wisps, he would end up dying in the swamp. That is where the saying "wandering Willy Nilly" came from.

Fishermen saw them bobbing up and down like lanterns and believed they were the souls of the those who died at sea and were looking for a place to be buried. Find even one bone, it was believed, and a soul would be put to rest.

Scientists call this light *ignis fatuus,* which means *foolish fire,* and have concluded that the phosphorescence that gives the firefly its light and causes the lights over the swamps are both caused by the same gas, methane. Methane gas, also, causes spontaneous explosions in deep mines. It is, curiously enough, the gas from cattle and other livestock that is currently piercing holes in the ozone layer.

Interesting as that may be, how did the Jack-o-lantern get its name? There is an old Irish tale that was found in Hatch, and others, that has been told for centuries. The story goes like this. Once there was a stingy drunkard named Jack. One night when he was imbibing, he tricked the devil into changing himself into a sixpence to pay for the drinks they were having. The devil did and Jack quickly picked up the coin and put it into the pocket in which he carried a cross. This trapped the devil so that he could not get out.

One day Stingy Jack, intending to go straight, gave his wife some money he had earned doing odd jobs, and promised to quit drinking. Jack made a deal with the devil to leave him alone for a year while he supposedly cleaned up his life.

Well, drunkards will be drunkards. As soon as he got out of sight of the devil, he went back to his former ways. Then,on the following Halloween night, on a lonely road, Stingy Jack met him again. Convinced that Satan was after his soul, Jack once again tricked the devil to leave him alone for 10 more years.

Then, Stingy Jack died. He was not allowed in heaven because of the way he had treated his wife, and because he had dealings with the devil. So he went to hell. When he arrived the devil would not let him in because he had pulled all those tricks on him. Stingy Jack said, "What am I going to do?"

The devil threw Jack a hot coal so that he could see his way around in the dark. Jack caught the hot coal and put it into a turnip he had partially eaten. And ever since, with this Jack-O'-Lantern, he has been wandering throughout the universe trying to find a place to land.

WHY HALLOWEEN MASKS?

Masks have been worn since the earliest times to ward off evil spirits and to coerce the gods of nature for favors.

Witches of all levels wore masks. People of all classes went to the Witches' Sabbaths. Because it was frowned upon by the ruling class, the nobility went incognito by wearing masks. The ancient Druids wore masks around Halloween to scare off evil spirits, ghosts and witches. Children simply followed the ancient custom, and now, when trick-or-treating, wear masks.

TRICK OR WHAT?

The custom of trick-or-treating is far from being new. Only the purposes may differ. In early England, the poor went begging for *soul cakes* on the Eve of All Saints Day. They carried mangel-wurzels they had turned into Jack-O'-Lanterns.

The Spanish, on the other hand, bribed the evil spirits to stay away by putting cakes and nuts on graves. In Belgium, the children stood in front of homes begging for money to buy cakes. They ate as many as they could because they believed that for each cake they ate, the suffering of one soul would be relieved.

In Ireland, according to Dr. William Madsen, professor of anthropology at Santa Barbara State University, the masked priests paraded around honoring a Druid god, Muck Olla, begging for food and tithes for the Celtic house of worship. The farmers feared what Muck Olla would do to their farms if they could not pay the tithes and gave nothing. Generally, their barn would be mysteriously burnt down or an animal stolen. Old Muck Olla would create some "Muck." In fact, that is where our term for creating chaos comes from, or expressions like "We're stuck in the muck!" Madsen contends that this practice was the forerunner of trick-or-treating.

Trick-or-treating as a threat used by little children to obtain candies is a relatively new phenomenon, perhaps just a few decades old. According to *The Folklore of American Holidays*, it appears to be an American phenomenon. Also, Cohen and Coffin, the editors of that publication, said that the idea of the Halloween sadist and all of the candy tampering fears were created in the 1970's. However they contend that the fear is unfounded, and that they recall warnings of poisonings as far back as the 1930's. They also indicated that the reports were generally "mistaken or fraudulent." Only two cases of death were reported in the 1987 issue of the Philadelphia Inquirer and one of those children received heroine from his uncle while the other was killed by his father. So it looks like we can stay cautious and alert and still have a good time.

Edna Barth stated that "Halloween, with more ancient beginnings than any other holiday, no longer has any serious meanings. Children have kept it alive because they love it."

Thank goodness for the children and the young at heart!

WHAT ARE HALLOWEEN PHOBIAS?

There is a fine line between folklore and phobias. For some it becomes difficult to distinguish the folklore of hobgoblins, pumpkins and fun from the black magic, voodoo and fearful superstitions that move one step beyond into the areas of dangerous rituals and harmful fears and phobias.

There are many sufferers of phobias around Halloween and there are many phobias with which to be afraid. The following is a partial list people have reported:

Samhainophobia-- Halloween -(fear of festival of the dead)

Wicaphobia -	Witches
Phasmophobia -	Ghosts
Hemotophobia -	Blood
Gatophobia -	Cats
Sciophobia -	Shadows
Paphophobia -	Graves
Necrophobia -	Corpse
Ochlophobia -	Crowds
Toxiphobia-	Poison
Nyktosophobia -	Night
Demophobia -	Fear of demons, devils & spirits

As with any symptoms of phobias, the symptoms can range from a mild anxiety over a sense of an impending doom, to full blown phobias with associated panic attacks. Hyper-ventilation, palpitations of the heart, sweaty palms, fear of loosing control or going crazy are some of the more common symptoms. The symptoms can do harm and cause a breakdown in any of the three main areas of our lives: the physical body, the mental and emotional, and/or the social or work-related areas.

Many sufferers go through all kinds of ritualistic behavior like locking and unlocking the door three times before going to work. Or circling the house eight times before leaving the home. Some will not even get out of bed on Halloween.

However, as I mentioned earlier in the chapter on Friday the 13th, people who are superstitious or believe in witchcraft are no more likely to be mentally ill than the rest of us. And they should not seek psychiatric help unless they are sure that the professional is an expert, otherwise, the sufferer may well not obtain any better help than he would from any other sorcerer.

People who had had previous psychotherapy and then came to the Phobia Institute and Stress Management Centers of Southern California were found to take longer to cure their problems than those who had had no, or little, treatment. Then, there were those who had gone to a psychiatrist to get help because they were having affairs with other women and feeling guilty about it. After treatment, and professing to be cured, when asked, "Do you mean that you don't sneak around and have sex with other women anymore?" they would reply, "Oh no. It's not that. It's that now when I do, I don't feel guilty."

Mentally ill? Not at all. Those people who have superstitions and beliefs in the occult cut across all social, economic, emotional and intellectual boundaries. There is no verifiable proof that people who are superstitious are abnormal in any way, nor has it been found that they carry with them a history of neurotic, maladaptive behavior. They have simply lost control of their minds, not lost their minds, and have lost control of their bodily feelings to the extent that they have hindered their ability to handle their actions appropriately. And it becomes problematic only if it interferes with their optimum performance, such as in their jobs or relationships.

Positive superstitions are *hope* based and not *fear* based like negative superstitions. Fear of black cats, stepping on a crack, walking under a ladder, or throwing salt over the shoulder are negative superstitions. Hopeful, positive superstitions include lucky charms, rabbit's feet, lucky pieces of clothing, various sayings, and touch-stones.

The Keying technique, as discussed in Chapter IX on holiday blues, is a system by which anxieties, phobias and stress can be controlled, and is not a superstition. It is systematic, measurable and predictable. It can be duplicated without fail over and over again. A lucky charm, like psychotherapy, is randomly successful, if at all.

WHAT IS THE DIFFERENCE BETWEEN SUPERSTITION, BELIEFS AND PHOBIAS?

Often, what may be one person's belief is another's superstition. Your belief may be my superstition, and, conversely, my belief may be your superstition.

It would be a good idea to explore the differences between myths, religious beliefs, folklore, superstitions, phobias and simple obses-sive/compulsive thoughts and behaviors.

Joseph Campbell, the famous mythologist, in *The Power of Myth* stated that the myth is "used for instruction...civilizations are grounded in myth." Myths and legends are stories about ancient ideas and beliefs, and often explain natural events such as the creation of the universe. The *Oxford American Dictionary* states that "The ideas then often form part of the beliefs of a group or class but are not founded on fact."

Beliefs occur when there is an emotional acceptance of a proposi-tion or a set of doctrines that is considered implicitly true. Beliefs have varying degrees of subjective certainty and are supported by assumptions, opinions, convictions and faith. Beliefs make an impact on the neurology of the physical body as memory traces or body memories.

These beliefs are codified into a religious belief. According to English and English in *A Comprehensive Dictionary of Psychological and Psychoanalytical Terms*, religion is a system of attitudes and beliefs, ceremonies, practices and rites by which an individual, or community, puts himself in relationship with his god, or supernatural world. It is usually a formal and organized system of beliefs by which a set of values are used in order to judge events in the natural world.

A superstition, then, can be considered a quasi-religious belief. Superstition is the survival or corruption of earlier religious beliefs now lacking in an adequate consensus from the point of view of a prevailing religious system or current body of facts.

It is tempting to apply superstition to any belief or practice one wants to condemn. It would be better to call a superstition a misbelief or an error, and when stubbornly held onto it becomes a prejudice.

According to some scholars, it is also a good idea not to refer to a superstition as magic or supernatural, because magic is considered to be a practice of attempting to call supernatural powers to bear in order to control events or people. However, the terms become confusing, even among the experts and they often tend to use them interchangeably.

One thing that should be carefully noted, however, is that in sociology and science, the reference to magic is not used if the practice is a regular part of an organized religion. The Hindu cow is not superstition. Prayer, also, is not to be considered magic or superstition.

Folklore, Campbell said, is used for a little instruction, but more for entertainment. However, simply put, folklore can be considered the traditional beliefs, practices and tales of a particular community.

Phobias are quite different. When a person is suffering from a phobia, by definition they know that they have an unreasonable fear. The same is also true of clinically defined obsessive/compulsive thoughts and behavior. The people know that the thoughts and behavior are irrational, but they simply can not control them.

B.F. Skinner, the founder of Behaviorism, considered any behavior or response to a cue, stimulus or situation that does not lead to a desired goal, as a superstition. That, specifically, applies to any phobia, or excessive and repetitive thoughts and behavior. So, anytime you find that you are not satisfied with the results you are experiencing, then it is a good idea to analyze what limiting beliefs you have that may be holding you back, or what decisions you have made that may be curtailing your desired progress.

WITCH HUNTS OF SALEM LIKE PSYCHIATRY?

Ronald D. Laing. M.D., in *Politics of Experience*, suggests that those gruesome witch hunts can be compared to psychiatry and psychotherapy as currently being practiced. Both the person accused of witchcraft and the patient being evaluated at the psychiatric hospital were, and are, considered guilty, or condemned, until proven "innocent" or sane, says Dr. Laing.

If the accused "witch" died, he was considered innocent. If he lived, he was pronounced guilty and was *given the punishment* and often killed. Laing, in describing the psychiatric interview, proposes that the patient being evaluated for admission to the hospital undergoes the same approach. If he or she denies having any problems in his life, he is considered to be in denial and is *given the treatment*. If he admits to having any difficulties, it is duly noted, and he is *given the treatment*. Unfortunately, it does not appear that we civilized beings have made much progress when it comes to judging others. Hopefully, our children will do better.

WHAT IS A GOOD FOLKLORE "CURE" FOR HALLOWEEN FEARS?

There are some very funny, fascinating "cures" and divinations surrounding Halloween.

One such "cure" advises that you be sure to crack all of the shells of your hard-boiled eggs on Halloween to prevent the witches from using them as boats.

Another ancient remedy is to hang all of your socks with holes in them outside your window to ward off the evil spirits on Halloween.

Put iron or salt near the entrances to your home and office to keep the goblins and witches away on Halloween.

APPLES, ANYONE?

Eating an apple a day may do more than keep the doctor away.

Since ancient times, the apple has been a token of love and fertility. The early Norse gods ate apples to stay young. The ancient Hebrew women washed in the sap of apples to ensure fertility.

Dipping for apples was a means of divination among the Druids and survives to this day in the folklife of countries influenced by the Celtic cultures.

The game of Bobbing for Apples or Snapping for Apples was once so popular that October 31 became known as *snap apple night*. When bobbing for apples, if a boy succeeded in coming up from a tub of water with an apple in his teeth, he was loved, it was believed, by the girl he loved.

When snapping for apples, boys would jump up in turn and snap at an apple twirling on a string from a stick. The first to succeed would be the first to marry.

Douglas Hill said in *Magic and Superstition* that girls could find out about their future husband by paring an apple and keeping the peeling in one long piece. Then, when thrown over the left shoulder it would form the initial of the one they were going to marry.

Go to your bedroom at midnight on Halloween, sit down in front of the mirror, and with another mirror at your back, cut an apple into exactly nine (not ten) slices. Hold each slice on the point of your knife before eating it. Look in the mirror and you might see, in the rear mirror, the face of your future spouse. And he or she may ask you for the last slice. (Note: if he does, give it to him!)

NUTS TO YOU!

At one time, Halloween was referred to as *nutcrack night* in Europe and the British Isles because nuts, as well as apples, were a big part of the celebration. Nuts, like apples, have long been a symbol of life and fertility.

With your love on Halloween night, do like the Scottish do. Put a pair of nuts, named after yourselves, in the fire. If they burn to ashes together, you can expect a happy life. If the nuts crackle or spring apart, quarrels and separation can be expected. (Over the course of history, I am sure that this has caused a lot of problems.) A brightly blazing nut means you should look forward to great prosperity.

Put three nuts in the coals of the fireplace. Name them; one for yourself, and the other two for admirers of yours. If the nuts burn quietly beside your nut, your lover will be true to you. But, if the nuts separate, that means neither of the named persons will give you lasting happiness. (Go get another nut.)

ASSORTED TREATS

Go blindfolded into the cabbage patch and pick some cabbage. If you pick a frostbitten one, look out for bad luck. If you pick a bright clean one, expect good luck.

If you want to find out who your future mate will be, put your name on a cabbage and hang it over the door with others which have been numbered according to each owner. When the person of the opposite sex enters on your number, that's the one.

Go to bed after eating Halloween cakes made of salt and salt herring without drinking any water. You will then dream of your lover giving you a drink.

Wear a mask on Halloween and you will have good luck all year.

Use the rite of the Norse god Freya, the goddess of love and marriage. She said to wash a fine piece of linen in a running stream. One hour before the clock strikes twelve midnight, hang it up to dry in front of a fire. At eleven-thirty turn it over and, at twelve, you will see the spirit of your future mate. (If not, you will, at least, have a clean piece of linen.)

If you meet the wandering Jack-o-lantern on the road on Halloween night, put out your own light or old Jack will come and dash it to pieces. If he gets close, ancient sorcerers say, "Throw yourself on the ground and hold your breath." (A good stress reduction technique.)

If you are lucky enough to be born on Halloween, you can see and read things in dreams.

On Halloween, melt some lead and pour it from an iron spoon into cold water. The form that it assumes will be prophetic of your future life. One girl who tried it saw the lead take the shape of a coffin, and her husband took up the trade of an undertaker after her marriage.

On Halloween, run around the town square with your mouth full of pins and needles. Come home, look in the mirror, and, if you are to be married, you will see your future husband. (If you don't, at least you are a darn good runner.)

Drop two needles into a bowl of water, you can tell by the way they move in the water whether you and your lover will come together.

Walk around your house, or around the town, three times with a mouthful of water. You will marry the first available person you meet.

Walk into a room backwards at midnight on Halloween while look- ing over your left shoulder, and you will see your future mate.

Look into a spring with a lighted oak torch at midnight on Halloween and see the face of your future spouse.

Look into the well at eleven o'clock on Halloween Day and your future will be disclosed to you.

On Halloween, catch a snail and close it up on a flat dish overnight. The next morning, you will see that the snail's slimy trail has traced out your true lover's initials.

Put corn meal by the side of your bed, and the ghosts will write your future in it.

On Halloween, if an egg placed in front of the fire by a young woman in love is seen to sweat blood, it is a sign that she will succeed in getting the man she loves. (so, be aware of blood-sweating eggs.)

CAKE MAGIC

This one was found in *The American Book of Days.* Bake a cake and put a ring, a thimble, a china doll and a coin in it. The one whose slice contains the ring will marry within a year; the one who holds the slice with the thimble will never marry; the doll foretells of many children, and the fortunate one getting the coin will be wealthy.

CAT MAGIC

Serve the person you like a love potion made of tea and cat's liver. That will cause them to love you. (Unless you tell them what they just drank!)

To become invisible, make a charm of dried cat bones.

If a cat rubs against you, you can expect good luck.

If it yawns, opportunity awaits you.

The cat that sits with its back to the fire is raising stormy weather.

Use the cat as a counter-charm. A ship with a cat on board will never be wrecked.

Never let a cat into the same room with a corpse. It, says folklorian Barth, may be a demon and turn the dead soul into a vampire.

These things are true, of course, because you know that I am as "honest as a cat when the cream is out of reach."

Play it safe and play it cool on Halloween. Give to UNICEF, the United Nations Children's Fund, and to the children who come trick-or-treating at your door, because those wonderful children are the ones to be profusely thanked for keeping the fun, happiness and joy of Halloween alive.

CHAPTER VIII

THANKSGIVING -

ORIGINS, MYTHS AND FOLKLORE -

TIPS ON THANKFULNESS

HAVE YOU EVER WONDERED...

... what the ancient beginnings of a festivity generally thought to be solely an American holiday were?

... why the Pilgrims of the Mayflower were called Puritans?

... why the Pilgrims chose to take such a long voyage to a new land?

... how the *courtship of Miles Standish* ultimately turned out?

... why we call a *cranberry* a cranberry?

... why most of the world's cranberries come from Cape Cod?

... where the *cornucopia* symbol came from?

... what folklore customs cause us to overeat on Thanksgiving?

... why some people are more likely to get into family arguments than others?

... how you can be thankful if everything in your life is not going well?

> ... what secrets there are for dealing with in-laws or ex-spouses on Thanksgiving?
>
> ... what a traditionally good way is to treat a wound from a poisoned arrow?
>
> ... what the best recipe is to make this Thanksgiving the happiest ever?

As the Halloween witches, black cats, owls, bats and jack-o-lantern disappear from our homes and store windows every autumn, there are pilgrims, a big turkey, multicolored Indian corn, the Mayflower under sail, and a cornucopia overflowing with the fruits of the harvest to take their places.

These are the symbols of Thanksgiving, a holiday which falls on the fourth Thursday of November every year. It is one of the most popular holidays in both the United States and Canada. Setting aside a day to express gratitude for a good harvest did not, as many people believe, originate in the United States. According to Hatch, the editor of *The American Book of Days*, the Thanksgiving holiday has its roots in ancient times and distant places. Many peoples have held harvest festivals to give thanks for bountiful crops.

ROOTS OF GRATITUDE

The ancient Greeks celebrated a harvest festival honoring *Demeter*, their goddess of agriculture, with a nine day feast. *Persephone*, the goddess of the seasons, was her daughter.

The ancient Romans paid tribute to their goddess, *Ceres*, who was the goddess of the harvest. The *Cerealia* festival was celebrated every autumn in her honor. Fruits, nuts and other harvest crops were plentiful and were a part of the feasts.

In *Turkeys, Pilgrims, and Indian Corn: The Story of the Thanksgiving Symbols*, Edna Barth relates that over two thousand years ago the ancient Hebrew people had a harvest festival called *Sukkoth*, the Feast of the Tabernacles. This Jewish holiday goes on for eight days, as it did in ancient biblical times.

Min, the Egyptian god of fertility, was honored at an annual harvest festival. The Pharaoh would cut the first sheaf of grain. This act, it was believed, would ensure everyone plenty because he himself was considered a god.

The Chinese, with their Harvest Moon Festivals; the Japanese and their field gods; the Hindu women and their goddess of the harvest, protector of women and others; the American Seneca Indian's "Green Corn Dance" and the Iroquois' "Great Feather Dance;" all are special celebrations of gratitude and thanksgiving.

The ancient Celtic peoples held a feast each year around the first of November, called *samhain, the* festival of the summer's end. It was a dual celebration honoring the lord of the dead and the sun god *Baal*. They rejoiced in the harvest, gave thanks that it was in storage, feasted, and remembered their ancestors by giving them offerings of food. (See Chapter VIII on Halloween.)

For centuries, harvest festivals were held throughout Europe, and in *The Folklore of American Holidays,* it is stated that in the "British Isles the ancient Celtic and Saxon rituals united to give us the time for the autumn merrymaking known as the *Harvest Home*." The last sheaf of grain was dressed as a doll and paraded through the fields to ensure good crops the next year and to give thanks for the harvest just in. In Scotland, the Harvest Doll was called the *maiden*. As scholars know, these customs were pagan survivors of English tradition.

"PURITANS" A NICKNAME?

Historically, as we all know, a small band of people, nicknamed "Puritans" because they wanted to purify the

English church from all traces of the Roman Catholic Church, encountered a series of unfruitful attempts at doing it. They then decided to set sail for the New World on the ship *Mayflower,* which is one of the popular symbols of Thanksgiving, and eventually landed and set foot on the famous rock at a place they named Plymouth, after the English seaport from which they came. (Not from the chicken that bears the same name.)

Practically all of their history is found in *Of Plymouth Plantation* written by the Governor William Bradford from what he called his "Scribbled Writings."

THANKSGIVING IN THE UNITED STATES

We have been taught that the first Thanksgiving in North America was the famous one held in the autumn of 1621. Homesick for their English harvest festival, the Pilgrims could not see a better time to celebrate their survival of the long voyage across the ocean and their first year of hardship in a new land. They invited an Indian chief whom they had befriended and who had taught them how to grow the corn which saved their lives. As the story goes, Chief Massasoit, with ninety other Indians, came to participate in the feasting. When he saw that the Pilgrims might not have enough food for them all, he sent several of his men into the forest and they brought back five deer for the celebration. They stayed for three days of merrymaking and feasting on fowl, deer, Indian corn, pumpkins, beans, fish, clams, lobster and, of course, the proverbial turkey.

This was not the actual first harvest festival held in the New World. There were three "firsts" prior to 1621. One was held forty-three years previously by English settlers in Newfoundland; another was in Maine fourteen years before; and the well known Berkeley's Hundred in Virginia beat the Pilgrims by three years.

The first Thanksgiving sports, however, were participated in by the Pilgrims with the Indians and white men alike displaying their skills at shooting guns and bow and arrows, as well as racing, wrestling, dancing and playing games.

The actual date of the harvest festival celebration in the United States was changed, by various presidents, many times. We can partially thank Mrs. Sarah Hale, editor of the magazine *Godey's Lady's Book* for making Thanksgiving our national holiday. It was the ending of the Civil War, and her persistence, that encouraged President Abraham Lincoln to proclaim the last day in November as Thanksgiving for the whole nation. It was later changed, for the final time, by President Franklin D. Roosevelt, to the fourth Thursday in November. Canada, thinking that was too far from the actual harvest time and wanting a three day weekend, changed its holiday to be the second Monday in October.

The American Thanksgiving, with its roots in former harvest festivals when people reveled in the feeling of plenty, has always been a day for sharing through clubs, churches and various groups to help ensure that the needy and unfortunate have a good Thanksgiving dinner.

And Thanksgiving is also the eve of our present-day Black Friday. Although the early Norman seasonal fairs were the beginning, it is now the traditional date for the beginning of the Christmas commercial season. This day of magic is used in our business community for divining purposes. The myth is that the consumer buying for the rest of the year is predicated on how the sales go on Black Friday. Who said superstition is dead?

SPEAK FOR WHOM?

The most well-known men in Pilgrim lore, Miles Standish and John Alden, were not even Pilgrims. Miles Standish was a red-haired, hot-tempered professional soldier hired to train the Pilgrims to defend themselves. As we know from Henry Wadsworth Longfellow's poem *The Courtship of Miles Standish*, Miles was afraid of nothing save making a marriage proposal.

The story tells of Miles Standish sending the young John Alden to Priscilla Mullins' house to speak for him. And, as we all know, Priscilla responded with this famous line, "Why don't you speak for yourself, John?"

And of course, as history tells us, John Alden ended up with the girl. Priscilla Mullins and John Alden were married, had eleven children and God knows how many grandchildren and descendants. Barth thinks they must number in the thousands.

TALES OF THE SYMBOLS: FACT OR FANTASY?

The harvest aspect of Thanksgiving is best symbolized by the ancient symbol of a *cornucopia* filled to overflowing with earth's abundance.

As are many symbols, the horn of plenty is surrounded by myth. A Greek legend tells of *Amalthea*, the goat who honored Zeus with her milk of life, broke off one of her horns and filled it with fruits, nuts and flowers. To show his gratitude, Zeus later set the goat's image in the sky. We know it today as the constellation Capricorn. Gratitude and abundance was the Greek theme.

We have the symbol of the horn of plenty on Thanksgiving Day, and yet we eat as if there is not going to be any food the next day. Why? Scholars in *Folklore of American Holidays* suggest that "food has an extraordinary symbolic potential" and that "the basic menu of roast turkey, stuffing, cranberry sauce, sweet potatoes" (spelled with an "e"), "mashed white potatoes and pumpkin pie" is just that --- symbolic.

The traditional foods elicit feelings of the very old, very rural and more "natural" way of life. It reminds us of the good old days back on the farm when life was simpler and more peaceful. Jay Allen in *The Journal of the Finnish Society of Antiquities*, is quoted as saying "that Thanksgiving is a kind of secular, nationalistic 'mass' where people eat symbols of their folk history, thereby regaining some of the qualities they believe their ancestors possessed."

Thanksgiving, justifiably so, is a day that reminds us that we are still dependent on the earth and helps us to renew our ties with it.

Corn, although not generally included on the Thanksgiving menu, is seen as one of its decorative symbols. The name *corn* means the hard seeds of a cereal plant, especially the main crop of a region.

England had its wheat, Scotland and Ireland their oats, and the New World had its Indian corn *maize*.

The belief in a Corn Mother prevailed for many centuries in Europe. Her ancestry as a harvest goddess included *Demeter* and *Ceres* of Greek and Roman origin. The belief that she remained in the last sheaf of grain from a harvest festival ensured her place in the Harvest Home festivals mentioned earlier.

By the time the celebration of Thanksgiving became widespread in America, corn husking was already a customary community activity in various parts of the country. One custom, during corn husking, was for the finder of a "red ear" of corn to throw it to the prettiest girl. He was then permitted to chase her until (heavens to Betsy!) he had caught, kissed and danced with her. (I wonder how many "red ears" were added by the elders to entice the huskers to work even harder.)

Both corn and pumpkins are symbols of Halloween, which have some of their roots in ancient harvest festivals, and are both gifts from the native Indians of the New World. But old Tom Turkey reigns supreme as representative of the Thanksgiving holiday.

Benjamin Franklin wanted the turkey to be the symbol of our nation instead of the eagle. The bald eagle scored low with him because it had lice, and, like people who rob for a living, a bad moral character! The turkey, on the other hand, was more respectable and a true native of North America.

And then there is the bright red cranberry with its sauces, jellies, and relishes. It is a must beside the turkey at the Thanksgiving dinner. Nearly one-half of all the cranberries in the world grow in Cape Code, Massachusetts, and according to the Cap Cod Cranberry Growers' Association, that equals 2 million barrels a year.

An old legend tells why:

There once was a certain minister who had a spell cast over him and was put in quicksand by an Indian medicine man. The medicine man boasted about his strong powerful medicine, but the minister said he had an even stronger brand of medicine, Christianity. So they agreed to a fifteen-day war of wits to settle the argument.

The minister might have starved had it not been for a white dove that flew over the minister's head every once in a while and dropped a bright red berry in his mouth. The medicine man had no spell against the dove, so he finally gave up, exhausted. The spell was broken and the minister was freed.

All the while this was going on, the dove would occasionally drop a berry or two on the ground. There they took root and started the very first cranberry bog.

Of course this story, says Barth, shows how strongly the Pilgrims felt about the only true religion - their own.

The Pilgrims gave this sour berry the name *crane berry* because its pink blossoms and drooping head reminded them of the head of a crane. With time and usage, the name evolved to cranberry.

The Indians used the cranberry as a poultice to draw poison from the wounds of arrows, for dye and for food. The cranberries were also used as a preventive medicine by providing ships' crewmen with vitamin C to prevent scurvy.

According to Barth, a cranberry may not be soft. Each cranberry that is used by the factories that make juice and sauce out of it has seven chances to bounce over a four-inch barrier or it is tossed away and not used.

From the big Thanksgiving Day parades of Macy's in New York City to Gimbels's in Philadelphia and the mile long parade by the T. Eaton Company in Canada, Thanksgiving is a time to give thanks for everything God has given us. A time for reflection and expression of gratitude and for a renewed connection with our Mother Earth who sustains us.

PHOBIAS? ON THANKSGIVING?

There are as many reports of phobias and depression around the Thanksgiving holiday as there are around many of the others, like Halloween or Friday the 13th. The symptoms of the "holiday blues" will be covered in Chapter X on Christmas. For now, it is suffice to say that the fears, phobias and depressions from which 95% of the population suffers, begin about two weeks prior to Thanksgiving and continue to two or three weeks after New Year's Day.

There is one serious phobia that is particular to Thanksgiving and that is *turkey phobia*: the excessive worry over being able to cook the bird correctly. Turkeys, anthropologists say, have roamed the earth for over 10 million years and create an annual occasion for collective national anxiety. Being a turkey failure is not an easy thing to live down. A San Francisco radio foodcaster, Harvey Steiman, said, "We're hung up on this image - if we don't do it exactly right, the ghost of Norman Rockwell will come after us." The symptoms of turkey phobia are dreadful thoughts that, at the dinner, all you will hear is how *wonderful the creamed onions are*, or *Oh! the beans are great*, or *Ocean Spray really knows how to make cranberry sauce doesn't it?* We all know what that means. The cook is a turkey failure!

Have you ever noticed that, at turkey cooking time, everyone will eventually wander into the kitchen and offer advice they learned from their mothers as to the length of cooking time required to make that perfect bird? It averages from 3-1/2 to 7 hours.

Mary Ann Hogan, in the Los Angeles Times, wrote that there is a crisis hot-line in Illinois called the Butterball Turkey Talk Line that answers over 1,500 crisis calls a day just before Thanksgiving from people who are dying to pass, for their relatives and friends, the Turkey Test. The supervisor of the hot-line, Marge Klinders, said, "We call it 'turkey trauma.'"

THE REASON FOR IT ALL

Something might be said about the spiritual attitudes of gratitude and thankfulness. The viewpoint of thankfulness is a holding in memory of something good that has happened, or an expectation that it is going to occur. It is similar to, but much stronger than, hope. Thankfulness is the period at the end of the sentence. It is the *amen* at the end of a prayer. In fact, Biblical scholars say that amen means "so be it" or "it is so."

With all there is to be thankful for, it is amazing how many people find it hard to be appreciative for what God has given them. Some have a lot of material wealth and have difficulty finding anything for which to be thankful. They seem to want more and more. While others, with very little, find it difficult to find anything about which not to be thankful. What makes the difference?

Remembering that gratitude is one of the most healing emotions, let us look at some very simple tips on how to become more thankful on Thanksgiving Day or any other day. Just the fact that you are reading this book means that you are here. Thank the Lord for that. I am sure if you take a moment, you can think of someone who is not. Pause for another moment to say a prayer for all those who have perished from fire, flood, earthquakes and war. That is a good beginning.

If your health is good, even if it is not perfect, then you can be thankful for that. If you are poor, or have lost your job, thank God you live in the United States. If you are worried about your country, give thanks for your concern. That is what has made your country great. At least we can hear the church bells ring with freedom.

If you are lonely on this or any holiday, give up that false pride and pick up the phone and call someone. Call a friend, a church or synagogue and make yourself available to help out. Go out of your way to do something for someone. That is guaranteed to cure the blues and cause you to be thankful without even trying.

DREAD THE FAMILY DINNER?

If you are worried about the family get-together this Thanksgiving holiday, and you want the day to pass without tension, you only have to pay the price of learning to give up. You may have to give up your resentment, your anger, your annoyance, your desire to punish or your need to blame. You may, also, have to learn to admire and respect you relatives. The rest is easy.

Any time you resent someone, it is because you are demanding that they should have been, or should now be different. If you are jealous of anyone, you are demanding that you should be different. Do not hold your breath for your parents, relatives or friends to change. They are not going to make the first move.

According to Webster's Dictionary, to forgive is to "cease to feel resentment against an offender, or to give up resentment of or claim to requital for an insult." In other words, to forgive is to let go of the emotional baggage and abscesses you carry around about the things people should have, or could have, done differently. What is, is. And it is your decision to dump the resentment garbage bag, or do you still want to get revenge? It is up to you. To forgive will allow you to change your attitude from one of resentment and distrust to one of thankfulness, which is love.

Put your resentment and blame aside. Thanksgiving is not the time to deal with that stuff. Make an appointment later on and then discuss it in a framework of caring.

And quit blaming others for making you do things you do not want to do, or for making you the way you are. Instead, take 100% responsibility for what transpires in a relationship and you can expect to improve the results.

Remember, they did the very best that they knew how to do. Everyone, if they live on this planet, came from a dysfunctional family. So give up blaming your parents for making you miserable. You are different now. You are an adult. As an adult, you have the choice of deciding how you want to view any situation. It can be seen as a problem, or it can be seen as an opportunity for growth. Choose wisely.

Changes in your own peace of mind will create wonders in your view of the world and the people in it. Hostile and angry people see a hostile and angry world. Loving and peaceful people see a world full of love and kindness, and are more thankful for their lives.

DR. DOSSEY'S RECIPE FOR HAPPINESS

The following are the ingredients for guaranteed happiness. I found part of it on a ceramic tile in an old restaurant in Redwood City, California.

Start with a good measure of kindness.
Add a dash of laughter.
Stir in an equal measure of work and play.
Fold in a big dose of courage to take a risk.
And top it off with a huge heap of love.

Thomas E. Hill, in 1878, wrote a very popular guide to letter writing, etiquette, and social customs named *Hill's Manual of Social and Business* Forms. In it he included a variety of tidbits and some toasts which may be found indicative of the flavor of some peoples feelings about Thanksgiving Day.

Here are a couple:

"Thanksgiving: The magnetic festival that brings back erratic wanderers to the Old Folks at Home."

"The Thanksgiving board: While it *groans* within, who cares for the whistling of the wind without."

And finally, a Thanksgiving grace as reported in the *Journal of American Folklore*:

"Yes ma'am, no Ma'am,
Thank you ma'am, please.
Open up the turkey's butt
And fork out the peas."

CHAPTER IX

CHRISTMAS -PART I

CHRISTMAS HOLIDAY FOLKLORE AND FUN

HAVE YOU EVER WONDERED...

... why must we kiss when under the lowly parasite mistletoe?

... how Christmas mistletoe and holly are used in folklore "cures" and magical spells?

... what the word "solstice" really means and how it applies to Christmas?

... why scholars think December 25th was chosen as the day of celebration?

... what kind of tree the early Christmas tree was, and when and why it become an evergreen fir?

... what some of the folklore legends say the ornaments on the Christmas tree symbolize? (Apples, candles, horns, bells and especially shiny tinsel)

... why we have the custom of decking the halls with evergreens like holly and mistletoe and what they symbolize?

... what some legendary and mythical uses were for candles and bonfires long before the first Christmas?

... how the name "Yuletide" originated?

... about the ceremony of burning the Yule Log and what folklore magic is associated with it?

... why Santa Claus comes down the chimney instead of using the front door?

... if Santa Claus was always a jolly little fat man with a red suit and reindeer?

... why we hang our stockings on the eve of Christmas?

... where the custom of attempting to be the first to say "Christmas gift!" originated?

... what the gifts of gold, frankincense and myrrh symbolize?

... where our word "magic" comes from?

... what the ancient meanings are of our Christmas colors?

... what the real motive was for sending the first known Christmas cards?

... if what is called the *Holiday Blues* actually exists?

... what the difference is between a phobia and a *blue mood*?

... what a person can do during Christmas to guarantee a joyful time?

The passage through many generations of observances has transformed the December 25 holy day into a holiday as well. The rich blend of customs and traditions has made Christmas in the United States a celebration of remarkable fascination. Although Christmas is the most popular holiday, in the Christian religion only Easter surpasses Christmas in spiritual importance.

Whatever popular, and pagan, customs have been added to it, it is essentially a time of joyous celebration in honor of the birth of Jesus Christ.

The Roman Catholics celebrate on December 25 and consider it a serious holy day of obligation. Protestant churches generally celebrate Christmas with a service on the Sunday morning prior to December 25th as well as on Christmas Day. Those, like the Russian and Greek Orthodox, who still stick to the old Julian calendar, observe the occasion 13 days later on January 7.

Although the celebration is customarily held on December 25th, the exact date of Jesus' birth is not known. Scholars say the reason is that Christmas was not one of the first feasts in the church, and there was no agreement as to if, when, and whether it should be included.

The story, as told by Luke, says that the shepherds were outdoors tending their flocks. Some scholars believe that, if this is true, the weather must have been warm at the time of his birth. Early Christian theologians chose May 20th as the date. Others favored late March or April, near the time of the Jewish Passover. Some chose January 1st, coinciding with the Roman New Year.

What does seem clear is that early observances were connected with both the birth and the baptism of Jesus, and they were held at different times in different places.

The actual date of Jesus' birth is still under much controversy even though December 25 has long been accepted. And modern scholars agree that it was chosen for the practical purpose of connecting it with the numerous pagan practices around the winter solstice to satisfy the people who were not willing to give up their earlier beliefs and rites.

HISTORICAL BACKDROP OF THE HOLIDAY OF LIGHT

As previously mentioned, December 25 has donned the social dress of a holiday as well as the sacred garments of a holy day. In its secular and festive social aspects, Christmas is a delightful amalgam of traditions of numerous cultures.

The overwhelming display of Christmas trappings seems to have little to do the birth of Jesus Christ. And, in fact, reindeer, Santa Clauses, turkey dinners, decorated trees, greeting cards, Yule logs and gifts are, actually, all echoes of the distant pre-Christian past.

These early festivities cut across several cultures. A number of ancient peoples believed that a solstice, meaning "a standing still," a time when the sun appeared to stand still and was directly over the equator, was a time of crisis in which, it was believed, the deities of the upper world fought the spirits of disorder and darkness of the lower world.

Special rites were performed by the early Mesopotamians to help their god *Marduk* battle chaotic powers.

Sacrificial offerings were made in the temples of the Greeks to aid Zeus in his struggle. When the saw the days begin to lengthen they were joyous that spring would surely arrive.

The wild and noisy feast of *Saturnalia* was celebrated by the Romans during the solstice season in honor of *Saturn*, the god of agriculture.

According to the *American Book of Days,* the Persians, at this time of year, honored their sun god *Mithras*, the god of light. This belief was much more popular in Rome than Christianity, and its followers celebrated the "birthday of the invulnerable sun" on December 25th.

The Jewish holiday of *Hanukkah*, which is also known as the Feast of Lights, was celebrated at about the same time. This holiday, celebrating the rededication of the Temple in Jerusalem, is still observed today.

The sun god *Horus* was honored in ancient Egypt by a festival dedicated to his mother, *Isis.*

Because all of these midwinter festivals celebrated the victory of light and life, it was only reasonable that because the early Church wanted to compete with pagans, it was vital to choose December 25 as the day to celebrate the birth of Jesus.

Many people have criticized any idea that the church fathers purposely impregnated Christianity with the various pre-Christian religious rites and customs. Jane E. Hatch, editor of *The American Book of Days*, writes that the majority of the missionaries who penetrated Western Europe after the decline of the Roman Empire followed the ruling of Pope Gregory I the Great. In 596, the Pope sent Augustine of Canterbury to England with instructions to continue observing the old "pagan" customs, and "to infuse them with Christian significance to propagate the faith, 'for from obdurate (stubborn and heartless) minds it is impossible to cut off everything at once.'" Hatch goes on to say that "on this liberal policy hinged the continuation of numerous traditional customs now connected with Christmastide."

Local pagan traditions combined well with the religious observances of Christianity as it spread in northern Europe. The winter solstice rites made their appearance as Christmas candles, Yule logs, and bonfires to aid the sun in its rebirth. The bells, greenery, foods, gifts and Santa Clauses are all expressions of the joy of Christmas.

WHOSE STAR?

The star on top of the Christmas tree has its origins in ancient times. There are myths about stars, and people often considered them gods. Early Babylonians, Egyptians, Chinese and Jews, all had stars that were important in their religions.

Scientists have many theories about the Christian star. Some thought that it was a *nova*, while others believed it was a comet or meteor. The most believable comes from the studies made by historians and astronomers. They conjecture that, not in 1 A.D., but in the spring of 6 B.C., the planets Mars, Jupiter, and Saturn were close together and formed a bright triangle known as *Pisces* that might have been the Star of Bethlehem. This would also shine new light on the day of Jesus' birth (no pun intended).

KISS ME UNDER THE MISTLETOE?

There is no doubt that the Celtic Druids regarded mistletoe as sacred. They believed that the missel thrush had brought the green plant from heaven, carrying it with its toes. That is how the "missel thrush's toe," said quickly, over time became *mistletoe*.

During the solstice, the season of both anxiety and festivity, they decked their homes with holly, ivy, and mistletoe, whose greenness throughout the freezing winter represented eternal life. They burned mistletoe on their sacrificial altars as a symbol of hope and peace. This ritual probably established the custom that enemies would drop their weapons and embrace if they chanced to meet under the mistletoe. Our custom of kissing under the mistletoe may have begun with this ancient practice. Norsemen, however, think differently.

The ancient Norsemen thought mistletoe was sacred because of *Frigga*, goddess of love and the mother of their sun god *Balder*. A Norse myth, previously mentioned in Chapter IV on Friday the 13th, in M. Magnusson's *Hammer of the North*, is a good example of various customs or fears connected with several different holidays stemming from one common source or ancient legend.

The myth, as you recall, tells of Frigga becoming alarmed because Balder had a dream of death. She thought that if the sun god were to die, all life on earth would die. Frigga immediately secured a promise from all of the gods in heaven and on earth, and every animal and plant, that they would not harm her son. She missed one plant, the lowly parasite, mistletoe, which grew on the oak trees.

The jealous god of evil, *Loki*, sneaked into a dinner party the gods were having in Valhalla, their heaven. Loki tricked the blind god of winter, *Hoder*, into shooting an arrow tipped with mistletoe at Balder. The arrow struck Balder, and the god of light was dead. The whole world mourned and all was dark.

At the end of three days of trying to bring Balder back to life, Frigga finally succeeded with her power of love.

She was so joyful that she began to kiss every one who passed under the tree where the mistletoe was growing, and she made a decree. Never again would the mistletoe do any harm and anyone who stood under it would be rewarded with a kiss.

That is why we, even to this day, are obliged to kiss anyone under the mistletoe.

Holly is another Christmas symbol that came from our earlier ancestors. The Druids believed that the green holly had special power because of its ability to survive the "death" of winter. It gave hope for the return of spring. A sprig was worn in their hair when the priests cut the mistletoe for the celebration.

During the Roman Saturnalia festival, holly was considered sacred. It was one of their favorite gifts and was used to deck their halls.

Because of this, evergreens were banned for several hundred years. But, as other persistent pagan customs, their use came back into the open in the 17th century.

The favorite Christmas flower, the poinsettia, does not have an ancient history. However, it does have an short and interesting one. It was brought to the United States over one hundred years ago by a man named Dr. Joel Poinsett, the first ambassador to Mexico. We fell in love with it immediately and it is now considered a "traditional" Christmas holiday plant.

Early Christians continued to deck their homes with the evergreen holly, ivy and mistletoe, and, it is conjectured, used the bonfires that will be discussed shortly for disposing of the limbs and branches. At this time, the legend was developed that the crown of thorns worn by Jesus at His crucifixion had been made from holly.

FROM BONFIRES TO YULE LOGS TO CANDLELIGHT

Christmas candlelight services came from the early belief that the light of the rising sun, symbolized in the form of bonfires and candles, represented occasions of joy.

The early Scandinavians built bonfires to challenge King Frost. With fire, the Persians honored the god of light, Mithra. The Romans venerated Saturn, their god of crops, by putting candles on small trees during Saturnalia. As we all know, the Druids lighted fires to welcome their sun god Balder and to scare off the evil spirits, but they also lighted candles on tree branches and burned a Yule log as well.

The Yule Log at Christmas also goes far back in history. Our word for Yuletide comes from the Norse *Hweolor-tid*, the name for the turning of the sun from the short days of winter to the longer days of spring, the winter solstice. Yuletide, like the Italian name for Christmas, *Natale,* and the French *Noel*, meant at one time the beginning of a new year.

With its roots in Scandinavia, the custom of burning a Yule log spread its branches, via Europe, to England. It was believed that all who lent a hand in bringing it in would be safe from the powers of witchcraft, and that once lit, the burning Yule log would drive out evil spirits. All kinds of magic built up around the burning of the log. If you touched it, you would have good luck and bad luck if you let it go out. Put some of the ashes under your bed and the house would be protected from lightning.

Hertha, the goddess of the home was welcomed by the ancient Germanic peoples during the winter solstice. With evergreens decking the walls, fir boughs placed on flat stones were set ablaze and, it was believed, Hertha would confer health and good luck to all as she descended through the smoke.

Barth says that the flat stones of Hertha's altar later became our hearthstones, and the fireplace and chimney symbols of home and safety. As a forerunner of later gift givers, she also set the example, as some say, for Santa Claus to use the chimney to enter houses on Christmas Eve.

THE UNRULY YULETIDE

England, in the Middle Ages, enjoyed wild, lavish Christmas celebrations. Christianity had spread throughout Western Europe bringing with it not only its religious observances but also the merriment of hunting and feasting, gambling and singing added by the commoners who were grateful for the respite between the harvesting and sowing seasons. This continued, from the first recorded English Christmas in

521 until the rule of William the Conqueror, who, in the 11th century, organized more formal celebrations.

The royalty was entertained at huge pageants with masqueraders dressed as mythological animals and other imaginary creatures. This was all organized and directed by the Lord of Misrule, whose merrymakers would often take over a town. His Scottish counterpart was named the Abbot of Unreason, and it is believed that these offices were formed in the spirit of the ancient Saturnalian Feast of Fools.

According to Hatch, impressive tournaments and feasts were staged such as the one in 1252 when King Henry III had 600 oxen killed and served with salmon pie, roast peacock and flowing wine to his Christmas guests.

"Waes haeil!" resounded through the halls as guests, enjoying their host's hospitality, toasted each other with wishes of "be thou well" and drank copious amounts of the steaming spiced ale from the wassail bowl. (see wassailing in Chapter VIII on Thanksgiving)

The serving of food and drink has, from ancient times, symbolized good will, even to the occasional appearance of a roasted boar's head served with tusks intact!

These medieval celebrations lasted from December 25th to January 6th (Epiphany) and, sometimes, all the way to February 2 (Candlemas). When we look at the feasting and celebrating, we are brought to the realization that holiday excesses have been with us since ancient times. Our seasonal over-indulgence and commercialism are not just a present-day phenomenon.

In Italy in 1223, St. Francis of Assisi was inspired to re-create the beauty of the Nativity scene as a way of teaching the townspeople the Bible story. Few of them were literate, so,in a natural cave outside the town of Greccio, he arranged live animals and real people around a cradle containing a life-size wax figure of the Christ Child. People from all over the countryside came to view the manger scene on Christmas Eve, a scene which became the *creche* which is still revered and used today.

"Christmas continued in much the same spirit until the 17th century," according to Hatch, and "the Protestant Reformation in the 16th century slightly toned down the Yuletide revels, but it was left to the English Puritans to push through radical changes in the season. It is said that they were alarmed by what they thought was a dangerous pagan atmosphere."

The colonists of the Plymouth Plantation in the New World, under its governor William Bradford, tried to stamp out the "pagan mockery" of the observance of Christmas. People were penalized for any frivolity on that day. And "no man rested all that day," according to Bradford's *Of Plymouth Plantation.* In 1659, the Massachusetts Bay Colony Puritans' Court enacted a law requiring a penalty of five-shillings for "observing any such day as Christmas." Town criers would go about town shouting "No Christmas!" The baking and eating of plum puddings and mince pies were considered heathen customs, and were outlawed.

However, the influx of boisterous Irish and Germans in the 19th century began to change all that, and, in 1856, the ban of almost 200 years was ended. Massachusetts finally proclaimed Christmas as a legal holiday.

In England, King Charles II renewed the celebration, but some continued to dissent by changing the name to "Fooltide." The observance dropped its wealthy, ceremonial garb and donned a social manner centered around friends, family and home. Christmas assumed the appearance it has today during the Victorian age of 1837 to 1901.

NEW ADDITIONS TO CHRISTMAS

Some new Christmas traditions were introduced by our pagan friends from the 17th to the 19th centuries, including Santa Claus, gift giving, the Christmas tree and greeting cards.

THE FORERUNNERS OF SANTA CLAUS

Santa Claus was a late arrival on the stage of gift bearers. We can see shadows of Ol' Saint Nick through *Odin*, the Scandinavian god whose eight-footed horse, *Sleipnir,* carried him throughout the world delivering rewards and punishments. *Thor*, the god of farming, thunder and war, was Odin's son. Thor fought and conquered the gods of ice and snow and was victorious over the cold with his weapon of lightning. He made his home in the far North, and his color was red. Almost sounds like Santa Claus.

The German gift giver was Hertha. Her gifts of good luck and good health found their way down the smoke of the Hertha altar, as I mentioned before.

Christians banned these and other pagan gods, but only in form. A legend grew around a man named Nicholas from Asia Minor. It is said that once there were three daughters of a certain poor nobleman who could not afford dowries for them. To save the girls from prostitution, the good Bishop Nicholas secretly left bags of gold near the chimney for them, one at a time. The third gift of gold fell into a stocking that was hanging near the chimney to dry. Some believe that this is why we hang stockings out for Santa Claus on Christmas today.

Anyway, six hundred years later, after many more stories of good deeds, the Russian Emperor Vladimir named Nicholas the patron saint of Russia. Italian merchants eventually took him as their patron saint, and placed three golden balls by their doors to honor him. The money lenders of the time were also the merchants, and that is why we have three golden balls as the symbol of our present-day pawnbrokers.

History tell us that as St. Nicholas was becoming connected to Christmas throughout the world, he, at times, carried a birch rod as well as presents. Sometimes he had helpers following him in the streets switching the young. This was symbolic as a punishment for idleness and misbehavior and was once part of the early pagans' fertility rites to ensure good crops and assist the young to have many babies. (See Chapter II on St. Valentine's Day)

After being banned for a while, he reappeared in Queen Victoria's reign. Santa Claus's story then goes through Lapland, above the Arctic Circle, where he picked up some reindeer and a sleigh, a sack full of toys, and set up shop in the North Pole. (Until the nineteenth century, he rode a donkey or a chariot in the sky drawn by horses.) But he was still seen as a stern messenger of reward and punishment with a broad-brimmed hat and a long-stemmed Dutch pipe.

It was, as we all know, Washington Irving who was inspired to describe Santa Claus as a chubby little man with a jolly smile being pulled by a team of reindeer. Dr. Clement Moore, captivated by the idea, in 1810 wrote the famous...

> *'Twas the night before Christmas*
> *when all through the house*
> *Not a creature was stirring, not even*
> *a mouse;*

Now, Santa Claus is seen as a jolly, rolly-polly gift-bearer and is loved by all children, Christian and non-Christian alike.

GIFTS FROM THE HEART

By the 12th century the practice of giving gifts had become common on Christmas as well as on New Year's Day. It was believed to have come from the scriptural account, in Matthew 2:11, of the Three Magi who offered gold, frankincense, and myrrh to the Christ Child. The three Magi, say some scholars, were ancient Mede and Persian priests. They were consultants to rulers because of their knowledge of astrology and enchantments. From the word *magi* comes our word magic.

According to Douglas Hill in *Magic and Superstition,* a wonderful gift from the spirits is given to any child born on Christmas day. It is the gift of psychic powers.

Edna Barth in *Holly, Reindeer, and Colored Lights: The Story of the Christmas Symbols*, indicates that gift-giving during the time that we now celebrate Christmas began with ancient festivals such as *Saturnalia.*

O CHRISTMAS TREE, O CHRISTMAS TREE!

The Christmas tree, as it is now known, originated in Germany, although its historical origin goes back to antiquity, when trees were worshiped as spirits.

The Egyptians took palm branches into their homes during their winter solstice rites. The Romans decorated pine trees with candles and trinkets during the *Saturnalia*.

During the winter solstice, the ancient Druids held secret celebrations in their sacred oak groves. The priests decorated the branches of the Oak of Odin trees with candles, cakes, and gold-plated apples.

Some scholars connect the Christmas tree with the fir tree which was hung with apples to symbolize the "paradise" tree of the knowledge of good and evil in 15th century German miracle plays. Taken by the plays, people began to put Paradise trees up in their own homes.

Still others believe that the Christmas tree began with Martin Luther, the 16th century Protestant reformer. Some say that while walking home on Christmas Eve, he was taken by the beauty of the stars twinkling among the evergreen trees. He erected a fir tree at home and placed lighted candles on its branches to duplicate the lovely scene for his family.

The Christmas tree was introduced into the United States during the Revolutionary War by Hessian troops who were hired by the English to fight the revolutionaries. It is said that they were homesick and wanted a taste of their homeland custom.

After Queen Victoria's elegant tree appeared in *Godey's Lady's Book*, the fashionable women's magazine of the mid 1800's, the idea caught on quickly.

In April of 1926, our nation's official Christmas tree was chosen by the U.S. Department of the Interior. It is named "The General Grant Sequoia." The giant tree is located in Kings Canyon National Park, California,

A Christian legend, Barth relates, tells how all of the animals, including cats, dogs and even mice, were allowed to peek at the

Christmas tree. All, that is, except spiders. One Christmas the spiders finally complained to the Christ Child about it and He let them in. After looking from the floor, they climbed all over the tree leaving their delicate webs. Then the Christ Child touched the cobwebs and they turned into shiny threads, like the tinsel we have today.

Today, with all its glitter, and the many Christmas tree celebrations throughout the United States, Christmas would not be Christmas without the Christmas tree, thanks to our ancient ancestors.

CHRISTMAS CARDS

Barth says that the sending of Christmas cards began in England when schoolboys, away from home, sent Christmas letters to their parents. These letters, it is recorded, were printed on paper that had Bible scenes on it. And in their best penmanship, in hopes of money and gifts, they would tell their parents of their progress at school.

In 1839, shortly after the introduction of the penny post in England, the true Christmas card tradition of sending cards to friends and relatives developed. One thousand copies of the card designed for Sir Henry Cole were sold. Usually regarded as the first of its kind, it was made by J.C. Horsley, a member of the Royal Academy. In spite of it success, the custom did not become widespread until it caught on in the rest of Europe and America after the English royal family began sending cards.

CHRISTMAS IN AMERICA

America's holiday celebration is a rich mixture of customs contributed by many countries. Although the gifts, the tree and the turkey dinner are now traditional nation-wide, certain fascinating European customs are still retained and practiced in isolated areas of strong ethnic heritage.

Ancient moving Christmas carols are performed in the remote mountains of Georgia, Kentucky and Tennessee that have long since been forgotten in their place of origin. Hatch indicates that the Old

Christmas Day, January 6, is still celebrated in sections of the Ozarks and the Atlantic coastline.

Our first clearly recorded Christmas was held in 1607 at Jamestown, Virginia, by about 40 survivors of the 100 original settlers without their leader, Captain John Smith. He was away on a dangerous mission of attempting to secure corn from the local Native Americans.

Christmas is regarded as a time for both fun and relaxation and religious observances in the South. These are embellished with the traditional Old World caroling, greenery, and the Yule log.

During the season of "Peace on Earth," the French settlers in Louisiana, specifically, practice the custom of setting off firecrackers and shooting firearms on Christmas Eve. It has spread to many other Southern communities and today fireworks are still considered a necessity on Christmas in some areas.

Also, traditional bonfires that burn all night can be seen in Louisiana on Christmas Eve along the Mississippi from Baton Rouge to New Orleans. They are intended to light the way for Father Christmas.

New Englanders with their Puritan heritage, in contrast to the southern revelers, tried hard to abolish the "pagan mockery" that was mentioned earlier.

The Christmas celebration, with all its ancient symbolism that reminds us of our common ancestors, continually tells us that Christmas is not just a festival of one specific religion. Rather, when we see the *Nutcracker Ballet*, and hear George Frederick Handel's *Messiah*, we realize that Christmas is a celebration of that which is deep within us all - the human feeling of life itself with its corresponding hope for a brighter world where peace on earth and good will towards all people is a reality.

CHRISTMAS FUN

Folklore similes have been in use for years. Here are a couple regarding time and speed: "He is slow as Christmas," and "Waiting for her is like waiting for Christmas."

Looks can be described as "It (also he or she) is lit up like a Christmas tree."

The turkey similes are "He is fat as a Christmas turkey," or "He is as full of... as a Christmas turkey."

The weather can be portrayed as "It is colder than Christmas."

The weather can be predicted with "When Christmas does no winter bring, Look for winter in the spring."

CHRISTMAS MAGIC

Count Christmas as January, and the next eleven days will foretell the weather for each month of the New Year.

If December 25 (New Christmas) is a mild day, expect a heavy harvest the coming year.

If there is a full moon on Christmas, expect a poor harvest.

It is not only considered poor taste to wash your bed clothes between Christmas and Old Christmas (January 7), but also it will bring you bad luck.

It is said also that if you wash clothes within three weeks after Christmas, you will wash someone out of your family.

If you hang clothes on the line between new Christmas and Old Christmas, you will have bad luck. (Nothing was said about our automatic dryers)

In fact, if you do any household repairs on Christmas day (or on a Sunday), the trouble will not be cured and may even get worse.

If a baby is born on Christmas day, it will be able to understand the speech of animals. (It was believed at one time that all of the animals in the barn talked on Christmas.)

Also, if you were born on Christmas day your life will be a happy and lucky one.

Put a pillow under the chimney to cushion Santa Claus's trip down.

Learn to say "Christmas gift!" very fast because the first one to say it when meeting another for the first time on Christmas Eve or Day, will be owed a gift from the other.

Carry a chip from an oak tree with you and you will have good luck. Bad luck will come if you carry one from a hawthorn tree.

Mistletoe ensures many healthy children if worn when getting married.

It is considered proper to kiss a person of the opposite sex while under the mistletoe from December 25 to January 1.

If you go unkissed, don't expect to get married the following year.

Feeding some mistletoe to your cows who bear calves during the holidays will cause them to be healthy.

Hang a sprig of mistletoe over the door. It will chase away evil spirits and bring good luck.

If the man wants to rule the house in the coming year, use prickly holly during the Christmas holiday. If the woman is to rule, use smooth holly.

Put holly on your beehives. Bees hum in honor of the Christ Child.

Plant a holly tree near the house to keep the witches away.

Jump over some ashes of burnt thorns and make a wish. It will then come true.

Keep your Yule log burning all night. If it goes out, expect bad luck.

Put the ashes of the burnt Yule log under your bed. That will keep lightning from striking the house.

If a barefoot person or one who squints shows up while the Yule log is burning, expect bad luck.

Give gold, frankincense and myrrh for Christmas gifts. The one who receives gold will be rich; frankincense, religious and happy; and myrrh, a healer.

Make a wreath from the last sheaf of corn and put in the barn. This will cause your animals to thrive.

Hay stolen on Christmas Eve and fed to cattle will multiply their health and make them more fertile.

Give your horse a drink of ale on Christmas. You will then have good luck.

Let spiders crawl on your Christmas tree and you won't need to put any tinsel on it.

Eat plenty of pies on Christmas. It is believed to bring good luck.

Plum pudding will do the same thing, but remember *plum* means to rise or swell and is not the fruit. In 1670, plum pudding was made of meat broth, chopped sow's tongues, raisins, fruit juice, wine, and spices.

If you like to imbibe from the wassail bowl, for good luck take some to the barn and wassail the animals. Then wassail your bees, trees, and fields. Wassailing on the Twelfth Night with a shotgun is a magical rite that will chase away the evil spirits and encourage good crops. And if they do show up, wassail them once or twice.

Play draw straws on Christmas Eve. The longer straw means longer life. If you are unmarried, the short straw means that you will marry soon.

Be sure to ring a few bells on Christmas. Their pealing will drive away goblins, put out fires, divert thunderstorms, protect you from lightning, and purify the air after an epidemic.

Roasting chestnuts in a open fire, named for the available persons you know, is a great divination ploy. The first one that pops will be the one you will marry.

If you are already married, put two chestnuts in the fire. If they burn apart or crackle a lot, watch out. If they stay together, so will you two.

PEACE ON EARTH AND GOOD WILL TOWARDS ALL MEN

The following is my personal belief as to what peace in the world would be like. It was written early in 1992.

WHAT PEACE MEANS TO ME

Peace is sublimely felt when, in my attempt to circumvent pain and attain tranquility, I move with child-like wonder effortlessly toward the alignment with the universal necessity of letting go and letting God. Then is when the turbulent waters turn to halcyon bliss. The stormy, ruffled disharmony is transformed into the tranquility of a sunny day.

Peace is the serenity a child feels in his heart when lying in the sun playing mental hopscotch on the little white clouds in the beautiful blue sky, hearing the birds, feeling the breeze on his face and knowing that everything is in its right place.

Peace, to me, is the feeling I have when I hold the realization that we are all of one family, totally related and interrelated, and that that consciousness is experienced as the positive feelings of unanimity and ecstasy.

Wadsworth said, "...for in all things I saw one life, and felt that it was joy."

CHRISTMAS - PART II

"HOLIDAY BLUES" AND HOW TO CURE THEM

The Christmas of today is seen by Christians and non-Christians alike as a time for fun, celebration, gift giving and love for all peoples of the world.

On the other hand, some do not see Christmas with eyes of eager anticipation and as a season of rejoicing. Ogden Nash, for example, is quoted as having said "Roses are things which Christmas is not a bed of," and George Bernard Shaw once said that "Christmas is forced on a reluctant nation by shopkeepers and the press." But, regardless of the criticism of our glorification of Santa Claus, our over-indulgence in food and drink, and the financial strain placed upon some by the commercialization of the season, many people feel differently.

Most people feel the stirring of excitement, anticipation and joy as the holiday season approaches. However, for some, like Mr. Nash, the opposite is true. Many suffer from what sociologists call the *Holiday Blues*. They begin about two weeks before Thanksgiving, and last until two or three weeks after New Year's Day. Based on my observations, I estimate that 90% of the population suffers from some form of holiday fear or stress. When these fears and stresses are severe or prolonged, an inevitable breakdown in the physical, mental and social life occurs.

The holiday blues, or fears, come in many shades. Let us look at some of these problems, some obvious and some not-so-obvious causes, and then offer some possible scientific solutions.

One obvious reason for the holiday angst is the high percentage of broken homes. Over 50% of the marriages in the Untied States end in separation or divorce. The children of these broken homes, regardless of age, often become anxious and fearful about hurting one or the other parent during the holiday season. Whom should they choose to visit first, or at all, on that special day? Newly married couples have a similar situation deciding whose set of parents will be seen first, that is if they are still a set. If not, then the problem is exacerbated.

On the other hand, the parents, more often than not, have fears of not being the chosen one. These fears often reinforce the parent's feelings of guilt and sense of failure as a partner and as a parent.

Some people become stressed worrying about seeing the family "back home." They worry about their appearance or how the family will have changed. Others are concerned about whether they will be seen as a *success* or a *failure* to their relatives and friends. Old rivalries are often awakened.

The forced joyousness that comes into our homes through the various media is often a painful reminder to many of the loneliness of their own lives. Scenes of laughing families seen on television, or in advertising, may cause hurt or bring feelings of guilt to the large numbers of singles or the elderly who have lost mates and friends. They are forced into an inescapable awareness of what appears to be the fullness of some lives, as seen in the Hallmark advertisements, as compared with what they perceive as emptiness in their own.

Another obvious reason is that often, because of the economy and the prevailing "hard times," many are feeling acutely anxious about the number, and cost, of gifts, when the most pressing item in their budget may actually be next month's rent. This is a major issue every year.

The fear of not having enough money to please loved ones, relatives and friends with expensive gifts, often escalates into even more serious problems when excessive charging or even borrowing occurs.

Then, in addition to worrying about the bills, distressing feelings about how to pay them later cause even more of a predicament.

A different aspect of the holiday blues is the sense of summation and self-evaluation that comes with the end of the year. Often, fears about being a failure, or too successful, can cause anger or guilt. As one year ends and another begins, it is often disturbing to realize that goals may not have been reached, desires not met, dreams not fulfilled.

There are often feelings of having procrastinated too much, avoided too much, accomplished too little. There is often a sense of not enough time or not enough money, which creates an overwhelming feeling that "There is not enough," which, when translated, means "I am not enough!"

Many of the fearful and insecure compare their own success or failure (financial, social and/or professional) with others. This comparing of oneself with others, often leads to feelings of guilt or envy or, in some cases, smugness. These holiday responses can hinder relationships, create stress, and escalate stress-related disorders. However, the suppression of these thoughts and feelings can, for many, create a sense of isolation and loneliness which, also, is fear based.

Some not-so-obvious fears and guilt surrounding the holidays are associated with family and social celebrations. Anxiety about a reunion with people who are not seen the rest of the year, often grows into feelings of guilt. Many feel they do not appreciate, love or even like their relatives and friends as much as they *ought to*, nor see them as often as they *should*.

Many people belong to what has been labeled the "Type A" personality group. These are often known as *work-a-holics*. When taken from the familiar setting of their work environment, with its associated pressures and time restraints, they often begin to experience anxiety and stress. They suffer from similar, if not identical, physical and emotional symptoms as those seen in people suffering from agoraphobia.

Just as the agoraphobic is afraid to leave the familiar setting of his or her home, the work-a-holic often experiences anxiousness, irritability, depression, and even panic attacks when not within the *Comfort Zone* of familiar work surroundings. This has been observed even when the pressured pace of the work-a-holic is excessively stressful.

Symptoms of increased anxiety, irritability, excessive arguing, or depression following a slow-down such as on a holiday vacation, are well documented. It has been observed that the "work addict" can even suffer withdrawal symptoms from the loss of the habituated surge of adrenalin which often, unfortunately, "goes with the territory" of excessive work loads. This phenomenon is the reason people often feel depressed or become physically ill following the holidays.

During the holiday season, many people are prone to excessive drinking and overeating, indulgences which seem to be more permissible at this time of year, in order to lose the holiday blues. However, rather than reducing these fears and the accompanying stress, alcohol, being a depressant, actually causes more fear and stress and worsens the condition. This increases the need for even more drinking.

So too, the rich foods traditionally served around the holidays can add to the blues rather than make things better. These excesses actually trigger the glandular *Fear Chain* discussed below and create even more stress.

Studies indicate that during the holiday season there are more people suffering from depression, feelings of loneliness and stress related physical illness than at any other time of year. Generally, all phobias are exacerbated, some associated specifically with the holidays begin to show up, and the number of suicides reaches its peak.

People suffering from *ochlaphobia*, the fear of crowds, for instance, find this season with crowded shops, markets, theaters, restaurants and streets, extremely uncomfortable. Even family get-togethers or parties that are large and noisy add to the distress of some.

Fear and stress are the primary factors behind any negative emotion, and the negative emotions experienced at holiday time are no exception. When fearful or stressed, what I call the *glandular fear chain* is set in motion. That is, the hypothalamus, pituitary, and adrenal glands discharge high voltage chemicals into the body, causing the adrenalin and noradrenalin "rush" that is experienced as fear, stress and pain.

If these demands and stresses are extremely severe, or last for a significant period of time, there will be severe physical, mental or emotional, and/or social or work related breakdown.

Finally, the rise in the numbers of deaths by suicide is only a part of the picture of crippling illnesses and deaths that increase due to extreme symptoms of fear, anger and depression.

According to Arnold Fox, M.D., Founder of the American Institute of Health, "Increased incidence of coronaries as well as car crashes is, also, a part of the dark side of the season."

THE WAY OUT

So, considering that holidays may be dangerous to your health, what can we systematically do to lose the holiday blues and enjoy a more healthful and joyous season?

Before discussing specific strategies, I would like to recall an important point I stressed in an earlier chapter. *What people think about and talk about, they begin to feel, and what they feel, they begin to do*. Thus, *feelings precede behavior.*These concepts in behavioral medicine are important to keep in mind as we continue, because the challenge I enjoy presenting to my colleagues is that in order to access desired physiology, that is, to generate the feelings we want, we must have some means of reorganizing negative thoughts.

CONTROLLING YOUR MIND

One of the many strategies I recommend for any problem is a scientific process I call the *Cognitive Refocusing Technique*. It is a systematic strategy for reorganizing peoples' thoughts or internal representations which, in turn, changes their feelings.

I have found that, generally, people suffering from symptoms of the holiday blues, as with any negative emotions, including stress and phobias, are focused in the wrong direction or looking at it in the wrong way. They are looking at the sad, depressing or anxiety pro-voking images in the mind. And some even create what I call *horror-movies-of-the-mind.*

These *horror movies* are usually guilt-stained negative pictures of the past, or anxiety producing thoughts of the anticipated future which, of course, are often associated with negative physiological feelings. Generally, people in this situation are also focused on what they do not want rather than on what they do want. These negative thoughts are often *larger-than-life* and perceived from the thinker's point-of-view. That is, people focused on negative *movies-of-the-mind* mostly experience these *movies* as if they, themselves, were right in the thick of things. They are unable to stand back and watch the "action" from a more detached, objective position.

One of the most valuable cognitive refocusing strategies I am aware of, is to realize that *we are not that thing which we think is wrong in our lives.* For instance, if we come from a separated home, we can realize that we are not the broken home, or if we are suffering from a shattered relationship, we can perceive that we are not shat-tered, the relationship is. If we are strapped for cash this holiday, we can step back and focus on the realization that we are not our bank accounts or the negative cash flow on the balance sheets. We can get out of our *horror movies and with* discernment see that we are only the person looking at a broken home life or the past due bills.

This slight alteration in point-of-view is a scientific disassociation process which often helps immensely in reducing the guilt and fears connected with a sense of failure. Then, re-focusing on activities that create pleasant, exciting physiological feelings is often all that needs to be done. Focusing from different points-of-view, that is, *seeing* it differently or *hearing* it differently will result in *feeling* it differently.

For those focused on financial problems, I think the cognitive refocusing thought that is credited to the late movie producer,

Mike Todd is outstanding. Todd, famous for his productions which included AROUND THE WORLD IN 80 DAYS, was a man who both made and lost millions of dollars during his lifetime. Dur-ing one of the down-swings, a friend supposedly asked Todd how it felt to be poor. Todd's response was, "I'm not poor, my friend. I'm just broke!"

We can also give of ourselves by being with and helping out friends and loved ones, instead of giving expensive gifts. We might find this to be a much more rewarding (as well as economical) experience. Love is measured by time and sincere interest, and the time we give is interpreted as caring. Sharing ourselves is the best way to be happy.

The sharing of self and showing interest in others whom we encounter only during holiday-time, can be an excellent way of reducing the fears usually associated with guilt and a sense of isolation and loneliness.

Maybe you will come back and report an experience as one of my patients did. After returning from what he thought was going to be a horrible holiday, he said, "Dr.Dossey, do you know that by showing interest in others as you suggested, I actually began to like some of the relatives I hardly knew. I realized I'd just never taken the time to get to know them before!" Even if you do not get the same results, you will still have the satisfaction of knowing that you gave it your best shot. Often, that in itself can be just as rewarding.

If you, or any of your friends or associates are going to be alone on one or more of the holidays, it will be beneficial to try to take a different point-of-view in terms of the environment. For instance, you might try calling your church, synagogue or some local organization. There are many places where one might go to celebrate with others. Possibly you might even find great satisfaction in helping others less fortunate than you during the holiday-time. By doing so, you will certainly be helping yourself. I guarantee you that if you take just a little time and go to a hospital and visit someone there, whether you know them or not, the wonderful gift that will be exchanged will be received not only by the one you visit. Rather, it will also be received by you for giving of yourself.

During the 21 years I have spent as a Marriage Family and Child Counselor and consultant to health care professionals, I have found that there were virtually endless cognitive refocusing strategies from which to choose. I recommend choosing that process which will most quickly, easily and predictably alter your or your loved ones' physical feelings, and, thus, your thoughts and behavior.

A somewhat more technical, yet easy to learn, cognitive refocusing process that I guarantee will bring you positive results, is to systematically imagine that, instead of being right up there on the mental stage or movie screen, pretend that you are in the audience. Look at yourself going through the negative situation *on* the screen or see yourself sitting all the way up in the projection booth watching that troublesome scene far below *on* your imaginary mental screen. This will instantly reduce the intensity of the negative feelings and will help you to see things a little more objectively. There are many variations to this process that might be added. For example, you can edit the film into single still shots, and put them back together backwards or mix them up. You can imagine the mental screen smaller. You can even darken the picture, make it black and white or blur it. Whatever is necessary to obtain the results to feel a detachment from the negative picture thoughts and internal dialogue. Generally you will, also, experience the automatic return of pleasant desired positive feelings.

CALMING YOUR NERVES

The Cognitive Refocusing techniques will be found difficult to implement when, neurologically, your resolutions or desired points-of-view are weak, or when the holiday *fear habit* is too strong. When this occurs, the holiday blues will continue. The re-focusing messages may not get to a deep enough level of consciousness, possibly because of physical tensions which short circuit the neurology and prevent the reception of clear signals.

If this happens, a different scientific way of attempting to access more relaxed, funfilled feelings is indicated. I recommend that my patients do something physical, such as, use systematic relaxation techniques similar to those described in Dr. Bensons' *Relaxation Response,* or meditate at least 30 minutes a day.

The act of physically going somewhere is another "do something different" strategy that makes you feel better. Taking a walk, which I recommend doing for at least 30-40 minutes a day all year long, will help flush the toxins from the body that result from anxiety and stress. But "breaking a sweat," not simply sauntering, will do the most good.

I also suggest that you remember times and experiences in your life which give you feelings of happiness and pleasure. Thus, you are re-creating pleasant memories in order to create the desired positive feelings. Using mental images of good memories is very effective because the body responds the same way to an image, whether it's external or internal, real or imagined. We have all experienced the awful feelings of waking up from a frightening dream feeling as though it were real, but knowing that it was not. I would like to emphasize that it does not matter what a person thinks about that creates the good feelings. The only thing that matters is that the images create the desired physical state.

CONTROLLING YOUR FEELINGS

After remembering times when you had the desired feelings, **and you actually feel them**, you can use what I call the *Keying* mechanism for re-creating the desired state again, when needed. This scientific Keying technique is done much like the Pavlov conditioning method. His *reflex conditioning* procedure was used when he taught the dog to respond automatically to the ringing of a bell. I am sure you recall that by ringing a bell (the Key), and by connecting that stimulus to the salivation response after smelling fresh meat, Pavlov, after only four trials, had only to ring the bell without the meat, and the dog would automatically salivate. This was done successfully with no New Year's resolutions, no medication and no psychotherapy. It was straight neurological conditioning.

For instance, think of something, anything, that creates the desired feelings. Then, like Pavlov, Key them in. That is, pair that feeling state with a predetermined stimulus such as touching your thumb and index finger together or gently squeezing your wrist.

When you feel that your memories or imaginations have helped to create the feelings that you want, as you actually touch your thumb and index finger together, say something like, "Whenever I touch my thumb and my index finger together like this, I will instantly reach this level of relaxation."

After four to six such pairings, like Pavlov's dog, this unique hand position, just as the bell did, will become associated with the predetermined physiological state of relaxation. Relaxation is not the only feeling that can be *Keyed in*. Feelings of being highly motivated, happy, excited or joyful are just as easy to generate and maintain.

ACT AS IF - CREATING POSITIVE FEELINGS

If you find it difficult to create the feelings you want strong enough, I suggest that an excellent way to make them stronger is to act "as if". I call this the "As If" Frame. Let us say you are attempting to create stronger feelings of confidence so you will not have to drink so much at get-to-gethers on the holidays. Ask yourself the question, "What would I be doing, how would I be acting and feeling if I did have the confident feelings I want?"

I mean that literally. Ask yourself, "What posture would I have? How would I stand? What facial expression would I have? Would I be smiling? What kind of tone and tempo would my voice have?" Involve and engage yourself in it completely. Then begin to act "as if" you have those feelings. Your unconscious mind cannot tell the difference between a vividly imagined and felt state and a real one. As you begin to get those positive, confident feelings, Key them in.

You might imagine someone you really admire, respect and look up to. See that person being confident, feeling confident and acting in a confident way. Then, become that person in your imagination. That is, associate into that person's body. See the world as you think they would see the world, feeling confident. Then act the way you think they would act. This will create strong, confident feelings in you, and you can Key them in.

You cannot think yourself into right action, but you can act yourself into right thinking. If you are participating in something of value, it will not matter if your heart is not 100% in it. Even if you are doing it because of guilt or coercion, it does not matter. As long as it is the right thing, and you do it long enough, you will end up thinking the right thoughts.

Dr. Harry Douglas Smith, one of my mentors, said, "Think as if you life depends upon it because it does." I would like to add to that, "Think and *feel* and act 'as if' your life depends upon it because it does!"

Often, when you are remembering something, it is as if you are sitting in the audience of a movie theater watching yourself on the screen. You're disassociated from — not involved with -- the scene.

If, on the other hand, you associate into the screen, that is, if you think of yourself actually entering into the "movie" as if you were there, you will find that the associated feelings will become stronger. You will feel more involved and more engaged. Then you can Key in those feelings.

Yet another way to increase those feelings you want is to listen to appropriate music, or watch the kind of movie that makes you feel confident. Determine what kind of activities make you feel confident. Perhaps you have a favorite visualization or prayer that gives you those feelings. Then actively do those things, and when you get the feelings you want, Key them in.

KEYING - FOLKLORE OR SCIENCE?

It becomes intriguing fun seeing if the Keying process, a technique for locking in any feeling you want regardless of what you are thinking or what's going on around you, is any different from some of the mythical folklore remedies. In other words, is Keying any more effective for curing anxieties, phobias and stress related disorders, than the rubbing of touchstones or a rabbit's foot?

The rubbing of touchstones, moonstones and similar things goes back into ancient times. Scholars believe that it felt sensual and good and the tactile smoothness would possibly calm people's nerves and make them more aware of their surroundings. Then, they would be able to respond more appropriately to the particular situation in which they might find themselves. It gave them more confidence.

Unfortunately, the magic of the touchstone and the rabbit foot, like psychotherapy, is often only randomly successful. The Keying technique, however, is a scientific method of predictably accessing the desired feelings. And it can be used successfully time and time again.

It can be used to create any needed feelings such as confidence, resourcefulness, motivation, creativity, decisiveness, relaxation, and the most important one of all, curiosity and wonder. It has, also, successfully been used by sports professionals, including Olympians. Overcoming fear, changing physiology to better one's health, creating attitudes that ensure prosperity, and attaining and maintaining love and loving relationships are some of its other functions. The most exciting use has been in the area of increasing people's spirituality and understanding and love for God.

The rubbing of the rabbit's foot, on the other hand, possibly came from providing its owner the feeling of being very lucky that he was not the rabbit.

Keying cannot fail. It happens, randomly, all around us all the time. If you have ever received a speeding ticket, you, no doubt have caught yourself slowing down every time you go by that spot where you got the ticket. That spot has become a random Key. After having had an extraordinarily delicious meal and a good time in a particular restaurant, you may find yourself smiling every time you think of that place. Again, that restaurant has become a very strong Key for you. Those are examples of random Keys. The Keying technique is a way to use what works randomly in a purposeful way for your benefit. In Appendix II, you will find more tips for Keying and Cognitive Refocusing techniques.

Another benefit and a further step in the use of the Key, is that the programming can occur at an even deeper level by holding the Key and the predetermined feelings, and re-running any memory-movies of the past that may be a problem for you. By this means you can wash away negative feelings associated with the past, such as pain and hurt from any trauma, while still being in a relaxed state. It has been successfully employed in treating rape victims, trauma and crime victims. Try it. I think you, like thousands have, will find it amazingly simple and incredibly powerful.

This procedure offers a much better chance of change occuring by adding new neurological pathways for past or even future events. You can actually alter your personal physical response history, as well as your focus or point-of-view for life. For a more complete in-depth understanding and use of both the Keying and Cognitive Refocusing techniques, you can obtain the 6 hour audio cassette program "Through the Briar Patch" and the book *Keying: The Power of Positive Feelings*.

The Keying process and Cognitive Refocusing technique work just as effectively with the previously mentioned work-a-holics or Type A personalities. I strongly recommend using the Keying technique to reduce the symptoms of anxiety and stress that might accompany the *holiday withdrawal* from the workplace.

Also, for the work-a-holics, by setting up planned events and framing the days during the vacation, the holidays will be less stressful and more exciting. Even setting specific times for relaxation often will give you a sense of necessary purpose.

For the *re-evaluation* stress, I suggest ending the cycle of old goals and reconstructing some new ones. This process of endings and beginnings releases the past and re-focuses on the positive possibilities of the future which keep one enthusiastic about life.(See the Chapter I on New Year's Day and how to make resolutions work.)

Moderation in the intake of traditional holiday foods and beverages is more than strongly recommended, and is wise all year long.

The holidays offer a wonderful opportunity for fun and games. Sharing some active exercise with family or friends or participating in some of the seasonal sports like skiing can help toward fitness and health and will chase away the blues.

Of course, we have all heard the old adage, "Physician, heal thyself." Now, whether you are a physician or not, with techniques like Cognitive Refocusing and Keying, this ends up to be a lot easier to accomplish than you might have previously thought.

Finally, something we all might do is take a moment to reflect upon the original purpose of the Christmas Season. Think of what an excellent opportunity this is to experience feelings of thankfulness for even being able to observe such a celebration.

So for patients, health professionals, and anyone, the holiday season can become what it was surely originally intended to be: a time of realization that the blessings of health and happiness are inseparable, and that the price for each is a sense of purpose, of service to others, and a never-ending feeling of thankfulness for all the great goodness of the earth.

God bless us all.

CHAPTER X

POTPOURRI

TREASURY OF SUPERSTITIONS AND "MAGICAL" SPELLS

When researching for this book, I found a hodgepodge of folklore superstitions that fell into no specific category. Many of the remedies, magical spells and superstitious "cures," like crossing your fingers for safety, stepping on cracks or throwing salt over your shoulder, were not necessarily applicable to any specific holiday. Others were so generic that they could pertain to two or more festivals. Some fell into the category of applying to none, and some to all.

So this chapter is a quasi-alphabetical listing of a conglomeration of old-timey superstitions, mythical origins, sayings, omens, divinations, "magical" spells and superstitious "cures" that I found intriguing, absorbing and often humorous. I hope you do too.

The information also comes from a hodgepodge of sources, such as *The American Book of Days; The Folklore of American Holidays, Funk and Wagnalls Standard Dictionary of Folklore, Mythology and Legend; Cunningham's Encyclopedia of Magical Herbs; Charms, Spells and Formulas* and others too numerous to mention. For more pleasant reading, their titles have been omitted from the chapter, but are included in the Bibliography for your reference.

CHARMS, SPELLS AND PREDICTIONS

Birthday spankings are echoes of multiple origins. The Romans held their *Lupercalia* spring festival on what is now our St. Valentine's Day. They had the custom of switching young girls to give them fertility and longer life. The ancient Germanic tribes whipped women and young people for the same reason, as well as did the Druids of the Celts. When I was a boy, on our birthdays, we received one spank on the rear for each year since we were born, and then "one to grow on, one to be good on, one more to live long, one more to have a good marriage on, and one to have babies on, and on, and ......on, and......on, and........."

Birthdays, as all days of transition from one stage of being to the next, have been considered somewhat precarious because, historically, any change has been considered hazardous. Birthdays were regarded as a time when the influences of the good and evil spirits had the greatest opportunity to attack the person celebrating.

The presence of friends and relatives, and their expressions of good wishes and love, is believed to help to protect the celebrant against the possible unknown peril during the transition.

Bees, for centuries, have been believed to have come from heaven. That is why we have traditionally used wax candles, as we do today.

Lighted candles have been used not only to aid the conjurer and sorcerer during life's changes, but also as a protection against spells and fits.

The ancient sorcerers also believed that if you watch how they burn, you can learn to use them to tell you about your future love life and other successful prospects.

To demonstrate your prowess, as we all know, blow them all out and your wish will come true.

Breath rituals are centuries old and are similarly connected with blowing out the candles. That is why gamblers blow or spit on their cards or dice before playing. Men spitting on their axe or shovel before using it may do so to improve their grip, but they are also following and age-old ritual of ensuring that the gods will make their work easier.

Cakes, for thousands of years, have been used in acts of propitiation and divination at times of special annual events and critical life cycles. Our predecessors, on the days of new beginnings and celebrations, gave cakes away as a magical means to insure fertility, good luck and riches as well as to drive away any possible evil.

Candles and other forms of light have marked all of humankind's occasions of joy, and birthdays are no exception.

Lighting of the candles was also used by our ancestors to ward off the evil spirits, and light their way to a long and happy life with their god.

The lighting of the candles also is a probable echo of ancient customs of honoring the beneficial gods, pacifying the harmful spirits, and for purifying and invigorating the fields (and women) before the upcoming sowing season.

Cracks, and specifically, the fear stepping on them, comes from an ancient fear of letting the soul out of the square with the four corners symbolic of balance and perfection. "Crack, crack don't step on your mother's back" is still practiced by the young, and for the same reason you should not step out of the squares or on a crack when playing hop-scotch.

Doves, especially white, have been the symbol of peace and friendship from ancient times. That is why we see them, by the thousands, released during the Olympics. Doves are believed to be the form taken by holy spirits.

Dove droppings, therefore, bring good luck to the person on whom they fall.

Earthquakes can be foretold if you notice the restlessness of your domestic animals, especially cattle. Certain people, called *sensitives*, have been known to be credited with special extrasensory perception that allows them to foretell the coming of an earthquake and its magnitude. Scientists are now checking the lost and found in the daily newspapers for the activity of cats and dogs to determine if they can increase their abilities of prognostication.

Fishermen must wear good-luck charms and allow no woman to step over their rods. This will ensure good luck while fishing. To appease the water spirits, throw the first fish back into the water, keep spitting on your bait, always bait your hook with the right hand and do not use an upturned bucket as a seat.

Gambling must be done with the help of magic of all kinds. Never gamble with your legs crossed or take a $2 bill. Both bring bad luck. In playing dice, throwing two *snake eyes* (two ones), is a "deuce" which is a euphemism for the devil. Allow no dog to sit at the gambling table, stack your chips in very neat piles, blow on your cards or dice, and will have good luck. If, that is, if you carry a horned toad's toenail and Lady Luck is with you.

Iron, and the **horseshoe**, like salt, according to Douglas Hill in *Magic and Superstition,* were used as positive magic to do good. The horseshoe is regarded as an infallible witch repellent because it resembles the shape of the new moon, the horned crescent. Witches and demons fear it, as do the "little people" who may have been the goblins. It should be hung above the doors with the ends facing up so that the good luck can not run out.

Ladders being walked under has been considered bad luck for centuries. And not because it might be good sense not to, but because ladders have long been symbols of a spiritual ascent to heaven. The admonition is, "Don't disturb those spirits who might be using them!" Also, a ladder leaning up against a wall forms a triangle, which is an ancient symbol of life. Therefore, breaking the symbol by walking under the ladder is dangerous.

How many people are afraid of walking under a ladder? British educators found, in an experiment, that over 70% of the people, when presented with the option of risking their lives in the street traffic rather than walking under a ladder, chose the traffic.

However, if you *must* walk under a ladder, cross your fingers, spit over the left shoulder (not the right), or keep silent until you see a four-legged animal. This will offset any evil or danger.

Mirrors broken, by sympathetic magic, will bring you bad luck. Primitives believed that any image of a person contained a portion of that person's life-essence. So the belief that breaking a mirror could injure or destroy the person looking into it eventually became the belief that just breaking it would do so. The seven years of bad luck following its shattering is a shadow of ancient Roman numerology beliefs. (See "shadows")

Salt, has historically been considered a precious commodity and has been used as currency. It was (and is) believed to be a powerful magical substance, and the spilling of salt is considered by the superstitious to be a dangerous omen. Salt is unchanging, and its ability to preserve meat from decay has caused it to become a symbol of eternity and immutability. It has been used in the ritual of pledge-making. "Taking salt together binds the two in eternal friendship.

Salt also has historically had the power to keep witches and devils away. Carrying a piece of it with you as a talisman is believed to keep you from danger.

Salt, spilled, never should be scraped up. Rather throw some over your shoulder and hit the "evil eye" to counteract the omen of bad luck.

Shadows stepped upon are believed to bring suffering to the souls of their owners. This custom is an offshoot of the belief that the reflection of a person in the mirror contains part of his soul.

Shoes have long been objects of magic. As a part of sympathetic magic, shoes and boots are considered good luck. That is why farmers' fences are sometimes seen with a shoe hanging on the fence-post. It entices the spirits of good crops to help them out.(Scarecrows, as cross symbols, also help) Throwing an old shoe at the bride and groom at a wedding or at friends going on a cruise is not just an act of jealously, but also will ward off evil and ensure a good venture and a happy voyage.

Sneezing, and particularly people's tendency to comment about it, usually with a "God bless you!" is recognized by very few people as a magical act. Scholars say that it has little to do with expressing your hope that the sneezer is not catching a cold or coming down with the flu. Rather, it stems from our ancestor's belief that a person's soul can leave his body through the mouth, and a sneeze may make the soul vulnerable to evil spirits by ejecting it. The blessing ritual supposedly counteracts that possibility. That is why the superstition of waking a slumberer or sleepwalker too quickly has existed for years. They might not be able to get back into the body.

Stars have historically been venerated as gods. That is why we "Wish I may, and wish I might" on the first star we see at night because the first is considered the most powerful and is more apt to make our desires come true.

Tombstones are used to hold down the deceased corpse, so make it heavy! Also, stones have been revered by the ancients and were believed to hold good and bad spirits.

Umbrellas being open indoors is a taboo that might be just plain sensible because of the possibility of breaking the knick-knacks around the house. But, there is also a clear connection between this practice and the belief in the ancient magical powers of the sun. The umbrella's purpose as a sun-shade gave it a special magical relationship with the sun. So opening an umbrella anywhere out of the sun's rays is considered dangerously offensive to the sun-spirit.

Weather can be predicted by watching your animals. Dogs will eat grass, cats will sneeze and lick their fur backwards, while your pigs will straighten the "curl" in their tails if rain is coming.

Weather is also foretold by watching what the ground hog does on February 2nd, Ground Hog's Day. (It used to be on February 14th which is now St. Valentine's Day) If he can see his shadow when coming out of his hole, he returns to sleep for 6 more weeks because there will cold weather for that much longer. If he sees no shadow, that is, if it is a cloudy day, that means good weather ahead. Does not make any sense does it? Well, I guess it does to the ground hog.

Wish-bone breaking from the turkey or chicken, is an old custom that brings good luck to the one who gets the larger piece. Folklorians say that it may be a symbolic carry-over of the old belief that there was magic power in the horned moon and the horned god of the Stone Age "little people."

Whistling in the dark, or at anytime, is not only a good stress reduction technique. It is an ancient way to summon the spirits to help you in time of need. Sailors whistle to create a wind. Be careful though, if you whistle too loudly, it is believed that you may stir up a gale. If you do, wear a gold earring, like some sailors of old did, to prevent drowning.

Wood. Touching or knocking on it is a common evil-averting ritual, usually done after bragging, speaking highly of yourself, or expressing hope for the future. This avoids tempting fate, or the spirits to puncture your pride or deprive you of your good fortune. The origin of this ritual goes back to primitive times when wood, especially the Druids' oak, was considered sacred, holy and very powerful. Christians have come to believe that it was the holy wood of the cross. Iron is also good, but has not been around as long. The Jews use the term *Cananhora* to get the same job done.

HEALTH MAGIC

A generous use of garlic or iron are overall charms for good luck and good health. They are better if carried in a bag hung around the neck.

Backaches can be eased by rubbing the back with goose grease or rattlesnake oil.

Childbirth can be made easier by laying an axe or knife under the bed.

Colds, according to ancient belief, can be avoided by carrying an onion on your person at all times. It might also be good for eliminating friends.

Cramps in the legs, or bunions, will be cured by placing your shoes upside down under your bed. Unfortunately, it did not say for how long.

Cramps in the stomach are easily handled by tying a red string around the abdomen.

Death can be averted, or at least delayed, by throwing salt into the fire if an owl hoots.

Diarrhea has been tightened by the eating of bread that has been baked on Christmas or Good Friday. Wow! Our ancestors' bread must have been as heavy as the proverbial cheese in the old saying, "That makes the cheese more binding." (meaning that it solidifies things.)

Earaches have been eased by pouring skunk oil in the ear. Skunk oil is made by boiling the fat of skunks. It did not say who is to catch the skunk. The urine of a mule is also helpful. Yuck!

Fits and **lunacy**, in case any of you happen to be prone to sudden bursts of madness, can be cured by planting peppers or gourds. Hanging a bag of peony seeds around your neck will also do the trick. Whatever you do, do not sleep in the direct rays of the moon. The word *lunatic* has a lunar, or moon, connection because more aberrant behavior has been observed in lunatics during the full moon.

Heart ailments are often helped with a substance made of foxglove, says old folklore. Like many folklore "cures" the doctoring was found to have some medical legitimacy. Foxglove is used by modern medicine too. It is called *digitalis*.

Herpes, once called simply mouth sores, can be treated by using what the sorcerers of the ancient Celts used: hazelnuts.

Hiccups can be cured by the ancient remedy of placing the thumb against the lower lip while the fingers are under the chin, and saying nine times, "Hiccup, hiccup, over my thumb."

Mandrake root has been used for various magical cures since Biblical times, as the book of Genesis reveals. Possibly because it looks like a human's legs and crotch, it was considered good for fertility, insomnia, as an aphrodisiac and a purgative. (One wonders if the insomnia and the need for an aphrodisiac have anything in common) However, a word of caution is in order here. Legend has it that if a human pulls up the plant, it emits an agonizing scream and the person goes instantly mad or dies. So, do as the ancient herbalist did, and use a dog to do the dirty work.

Night sweats can be stopped by placing a pan of water under the bed.

Phobias are arrested in many ways. Aristotle recommended garlic for the cure of hydrophobia, the fear of water or swimming. For an overall cure for phobias, according to the Celts, lavender is good. Elder or Devil's eye, according to the ancient Norse sorcerers, exorcises negative spirits. Courage oil made from rosemary, five-finger grass, gardenia petals, and a small piece of High John the Conqueror root does wonders scaring fear away.

Phobias like arachibutyrophobia, the fear of getting peanut butter stuck to the roof of your mouth, can be cured by mixing an ample amount of honey with it. On one occasion, my beautiful wife, Lois, and I were talking with country music star Cliffie Stone and his lovely wife Joan Carol, friends and authors of *Everything You Wanted to Know About Songwriting and Didn't Know Who to Ask*. I was telling them about how 27 million people were afraid of *leaving* the house because of having *agoraphobia*. Cliffie promptly added, "That's nothing Donald, there are 29 million people who suffer from *nagraphobia*." After I curiously asked what that was, he replied, "The fear of *going* home at night."

Rheumatism can be cured, as can other problems, by carrying a nail from a horseshoe with you.

Toothaches can be taken care of by carrying, by the teeth, the skull or jawbone of a horse as far as is possible in complete secrecy. (I should hope so.)

Venereal disease, if you happen to be afraid of it, can be prevented, or cured. Wearing a copper wire around your leg or arm has been found helpful.

Warts are best handled by being "bought" from you by someone else. But, washing them in stump water at midnight, under a full moon, is also believed to be good. If those do not work, wash the wart with stolen bacon, then bury the bacon.

Whooping cough can be cured by mixing chopped garlic in lard, spreading it on brown paper, and fastening that to the sufferer's feet. If that does not help, you might try another folklore "cure" of hare's milk, or milk drunk out of a dish from which a fox has previously drunk. This stems from the belief in the witches' power to change themselves into a fox when they are not using the form of cats, bats, toads or spiders.

SEX, LOVE AND MARRIAGE

It is good to plant marigolds in the soil on which your desired love has stepped. As the flowers bloom, your choice will begin to love you. Marigolds, for ages, have been considered magical because they follow the sun and therefore partake of its power.

A woman should steal a man's hatband and wear it as a garter. This will ensure her his love.

Carry the beard of a wild turkey and you will attract love.

When walking with a friend or lover, let nothing, like posts or a fire hydrant, come between you, and you will keep the love or friendship strong. As a boy, I can remember that if it did happen, who ever said first "Jinx, you owe me a coke" would be owed one by the other person. Lois, my love, was taught to say "Bread and Butter!"

Rice is thrown at newly married couples to transfer the power of earth's fertility contained in the rice to them. Thank God we live here. In other cultures people are known to throw grain, nuts, fruit or cake. We stopped throwing cake and started serving it to everyone instead, but for the same reason: fertility.

Weddings in the month of May have been considered unlucky since Roman times because it was their month to honor the dead. June is our most popular month. Perhaps it is connected with spring mating instincts or just to avoid May.

Wedding garters for a bride must be blue to follow the ancient symbol of constancy and spirituality.

When throwing her wedding bouquet to the unmarried women, the bride is practicing an ancient custom in which it is believed that whoever catches it, will marry that year.

Wedding rings are the most prominent superstitious feature of the ceremony. They go back to the ancient Egyptians and their betrothal vows. Never take one off unless you are using it to fight off a witch. Then it is OK.

The wedding practice of carrying the bride across the threshold, scholars contend, is possibly a remnant of the old custom of marriage by capture. Or it could be from the fear of stumbling on the threshold, because stumbling is widely held to be a bad omen.

The terms *bridesmaids* and *bestman* are also believed by some to be vestiges of the *marriage by capture* theme. They could represent the two contending families fighting it out while the abduction was taking place.

The word *groom* is used because the man is thought to be the servant and is supposed wait on the bride. Ladies, take heed.

The term *honeymoon* comes from the belief that the family *and* the bride and groom were to drink only mead liquor made of honey for a period of one month, or a moon. Perhaps that was to loosen up the newlyweds for fertility purposes.

To ensure having a child with the sex of your choosing, Douglas Hill says to do as they do in France. The husband is to stick a knife in his pregant wife's mattress for a boy and put a skillet under her bed for a girl. The sexual symbolism is obvious.

In the Ozarks of America, it is recommended that the father-to-be sit on the roof near the chimney for seven hours to produce a boy. It might be better to stay in bed with the bride for seven hours, but who knows.

If a wife is having trouble getting pregnant, it is suggested that she go naked in her garden on Midsummer's Eve (June 23) and pick the yellow flower called St.-John's-wort.

We humans are, no doubt, superstitious by nature, and, I hope, will never become too reasonable or logical. We have not as yet. I hope we never do because, found in our world of love, music, art, theater and faith in a higher power, are all of the enriching and rewarding experiences of life which come from a different and, I believe, a higher truth.

Our folklorian historians of the future will not lack any material from which new collections of superstition, magic, omens and divinations can be made. When they begin to study us and our present-day lives, the attempt to comprehend what new forms the ancient beliefs and rituals have taken may provide their biggest problem. But, I am sure they will succeed. As we adapt to new environments, there is no doubt that we will take our ancestors with us, one way or another. I pray that we never forget our ancestors, nor forsake them and their love, as we move ahead toward making this planet a more loving place in which to live.

APPENDIX I

FOLKLORE RECIPES

WASSAIL BOWL (24 Cups) *Non-alcoholic*

- 1 gallon Apple Cider
- 1 cup light or Brown Sugar
- 1 6-ounce can frozen Lemonade Concentrate
- 1 6-ounce can frozen Orange Concentrate
- 1 Tablespoon Whole Cloves
- 1 Tablespoon Whole Allspice
- 1 teaspoon ground Nutmeg
- 24 long Cinnamon Sticks

Directions: Combine Cider, Brown Sugar, undiluted Lemonade & Orange Juice Concentrate. Put Cloves & Allspice in Cheesecloth. Add to Cider with Nutmeg. Simmer covered for 20 minutes. Remove bag. Place Cinnamon Sticks in cups. Serve.

CRANBERRY CHUTNEY (4 Cups)

1 pound Cranberries

1/4 cup Raisins

1/2 cup Honey

1/2 cup frozen Apple Juice Concentrate

6 Tablespoons Cider Vinegar

1/4 cup Bottled Water

1-2 Tablespoons minced Fresh Ginger

1/2 teaspoon ground Allspice

2 sticks Cinnamon

1/4 teaspoon Cayenne Pepper

1 Onion, diced

2 Green Apples, peeled, cored and diced

Directions: Combine first 6 ingredients, and cook over medium heat until berries begin to pop, about 10 minutes. Add remaining ingredients, and cook 40 minutes. Refrigerate in airtight jar. Mixture may be frozen.

CRANBERRY SAUCE, Spiced (4 1/2 Cups)

2 cups Water

2 cups Sugar

2 Tablespoons grated Orange rind

2 pounds fresh or frozen Cranberries

2 long Cinnamon Sticks

4 Whole Cloves

Directions: As you stir to dissolve sugar, bring water and sugar to a boil. Add cranberries, bring to a boil and reduce heat and boil uncovered very gently for 10 minutes. Stir occasionally lovingly and tenderly. Add orange rind when cranberries are cooked. Stir in cinnamon sticks and whole cloves (or put in a cheesecloth bag) with a caring hand. Remove from heat and let cool in room temperature. Remove bag and refrigerate. Serve with love.

T.I.P.S. - COGNITIVE REFOCUSING

APHORISMS AND TIPS FOR COGNITIVE REFOCUSING

1. Make it OK to control your mind.
2. Acknowledge and believe you are not your mind. You are the one observing the mind.
3. Know it's not what happens outside. Rather, it's how you react inside your mind that determines how you feel and what you do.
4. Realize it's not *what* you think but *how* you think that makes a difference in what you feel and what you do. That is, how big and how close are your mental images or how loud your internal self talk.
5. Remember, the bigger and closer or louder your thoughts the stronger and more intense the associated feelings and actions.
6. Develop Attitudes, Frames of Mind, Points-of View that are held by people who can control their minds. Consciously hold these presup positions or frames until they become habits.
7. Practice holding a mental image of yourself being 10 feet tall for three minutes per day for two weeks. This will automatically increase your self-image and self worth.
8. Practice a Relaxation Technique or some form of Meditation daily. This will help you to become the Observer or Witness.

PRESUPPOSITIONS FOR MIND CONTROL AND COGNITIVE REFOCUSING.

1. I can think anything I want, watching and listening with curiosity and wonder. The unconscious mind will let me know with discern ment, when to act on these thoughts.
2. I am now in full control of my thoughts /feelings/actions.
3. I am making a conscious contact with God daily.
4. I am practicing the Cognitive Refocusing techniques every day.
5. I am giving thanks to all "stumbling blocks" until they turn into positive learnings and understandings.

Appendix II

T.I.P.S. - KEYING

LETTING GO OF THE PAST AND REROUTING YOUR FUTURE

WHAT DOESN'T WORK PREDICTABLY:

Psychotherapy • Visualizations • Positive Thinking • Desires
Understanding • Logic & Reason • Will Power • Motivational Talks

KEY: The Key is a pre-determined stimulus that can unlock any Body Memories you want.

KEYING: A way to predictably "lock in" and "unlock" any feelings you want regardless of what you are thinking or what is going on around you.

STEPS IN KEYING:

1. Determine what your Key will be.
2. Acknowledge what you are feeling or experiencing.
3. Decide what you want to feel instead.
4. Ask yourself "Have I ever had a time when I felt the way I want to feel?"
5. Remember that time. (Mind and Body never forget.)
6. Key it in (Pair them up by pressing your Key when the desired state is felt.)

7. Stack the Key by repeating step 6 several times.

8. Test the Key by holding it. The desired feelings will return within 2 to 7 seconds.

9. Applications: Present, letting go of the Past and rerouting the Future.

WASHING AWAY PAST BODY MEMORIES:

(Letting Go of the Past.)

1. Test negative past Key. (Identify past experience to be washed.)

2. Hold new positive Key.

3. From audience point of view, hold new positive Key.

4. Review negative past memories.

5. Test results. (Let go of Key and think of negative past experience.)

When completed you will feel PEACE, ASSURANCE, FORGIVE-NESS, COMPASSION, UNDERSTANDING, GRATITUDE and LOVE.

FUTURE PACING:

Redirecting your future predictably (A researched technique, beyond visualization, that works.)

1. Acknowledge current situation.

2. Give thanks for the "problem."

3. Determine what you want instead.

4. See, hear, and *feel* the desired experience holding your "As If" Key, then

5. Begin with present and progress to one week, one month and one year seeing yourself feeling and doing what you want to do.

6. Test your work by thinking of future situation or actually going there.

7. Get out of the way and KEEP EYES OPEN for the "DELI SIGNS" of progress.

Those who are curious and want a more in-depth and guided way of using Keying for the present, past and future, may call and order the book *Keying: The Power of Positive Feelings* or cassette tapes "THROUGH THE BRIAR PATCH."

DR. DOSSEY'S FEAR AND PHOBIA FINDER

WHAT IS A PHOBIA?

The classical definition of a Phobic Disorder is, "...irrational, persistent fear of or an excessive avoidance of a specific object, some particular activity or situation."

The American Psychiatric Association subdivides Phobic Disorders into three types:

1. Agoraphobia: fear of open spaces, the most common and severe of phobias.
2. Social Phobia: fear of embarrassment or ridicule in social situations.
3. Simple Phobia: fear of specific discreet objects, situations or activities.

All three types can manifest with or without panic attacks.

The following is a *partial* list of these three subdivisions:

AGORAPHOBIA: Fear of....

Crowded spaces
Leaving familiar settings
Stores
Elevators
Leaving Home
Public transportation
Leaving place of business
Markets
Losing a loved one
Churches & Synagogues

Theaters
Moving
Traveling in automobiles
Being alone
Change of neighborhood
Flying
Change of job
Driving on freeway
Traveling on trains, buses,
boats, etc.

SOCIAL PHOBIA: Fear of...

Ridicule
Being laughed at
Losing Face
Blushing
Embarrassment
Delegating authority
Eating in public alone
Talking to superiors
Assuming responsibility

Job security
Social functions
Failure
Financial security
Public speaking
Success
Writing for publications
Promotions

SIMPLE PHOBIA: Fear of...

AIDS
Air
Animals
Auroral lights

Nosophobia
Aerophobia
Zoophobia
Auroraphobia

Bacteria	Bacteriophobia, Microbiophobia
Beards	Pogonophobia
Bees	Apiphobia, Melissephobia
Being afraid	Phobophobia
Being alone	Agoraphobia, Monophobia, Eremophobia
Being beaten	Rhobdophobia
Being bound	Merinthophobia
Being buried alive	Taphophobia
Being dirty	Automysophobia
Being found out as Imposter	Imponereophobia
Being egotistical	Autophobia
Being scratched	Amychophobia
Being stared at	Scopophobia
Birds	Ornithophobia
Blood	Hematophobia
Blushing	Ereuthophobia
Books	Bibliophobia
Cancer	Cancerophobia, Carcinomatophobia
Cats	Gatophobia
Certain name	Onomatophobia
Change, moving	Tropophobia
Chickens	Alektorophobia
Childbirth	Tocophobia
Children	Pediophobia
China	Sinophobia
Choking	Pnigophobia
Cholera	Cholerophobia
Churches	Ecclestaphobia
Clouds	Nephophobia
Cold	Psychrophobia, Frigophobia

Colors	Chromatophobia
Computers	Technophobia, Computophobia
Corpse	Neerophobia
Crossing a bridge	Gephyrophobia
Crowds	Ochilophobia
Crystals	Crystallophobia
Dampness	Hygrophobia
Dawn	Eosophobia
Daylight	Phengophobia
Death	Necrophophobia
Decision-making	Decidophobia
Deformity	Dysmorphophobia
Demons, devils	Demonophobia
Dentists	Densophobia
Depth	Bathophobia
Dirt	Mysophobia, Rhypophobia
Disease	Nosophobia, Pathophobia
Disorder	Ataxiophobia
Doctors	Iatophobia
Dogs	Cynophobia
Dolls	Pediophobia
Draught	Anemophobia
Dreams	Oneirophobia
Drink	Potophobia
Drinking	Dipsophobia
Driving on expressway	Dronophobia
Drugs	Pharmacophobia
Duration	Chronophobia
Dust	Amathophobia
Earthquakes	Seismosophobia, Seismophobia
Electricity	Electrophobia
Elevated places, heights	Acropbobia
Empty rooms	Kenophobia

Enclosed space	Claustrophobia
England and things English	Anglophobia
Everything	Panophobia, Panphobia
Eyes	Ommatophobia
Faces	Coprophobia
Failure	Kakorraphiaphobia
Fatigue	Ponopholia
Fear	Phobopbia
Feathers	Preronophobia
Fire	Pyrophobia
Fish	Iclathyophobia
Flashes	Selaphobia
Flogging	Mastigophobia
Flood	Anthophobia
Flowers	Anthophobia
Flute	Anlophobia
Flying	Aerophobia
Fog	Homichlophobia
Food	Shophobia, Cibophobia
Foreigners	Zenophobia, Xenophobia
France and things French	Gallophobia
Freedom	Eleutherophobia
Friday the 13th	Paraskavedekatriaphobia
Fur	Doraphobia
Gaiety	Cherophobia
Germany and things German	Germanophobia
Germs	Spermophobia
Ghosts	Phasmophobia
Glass	Crystallophobia, Hyalophobia
God	Theophobia
Going home	Nagraphobia
Going to bed	Clinophobia
Grave	Taphophobia

Gravity	Barophobia
Hair	Chaetophobia
Halloween	Shamhainophobia
Head being too big	Larguscaputophobia
Heart disease	Cardiophobia
Heat	Thermophobia
Heaven	Ouranophobia
Heights	Acrophobia
Heredity	Patroiophobia
Home surroundings	Ecophobia, Oikophobia
Home	Donatophobia
Horses	Hippophobia
Human beings	Anthropophobia
Ice, frost	Cryophobia
Ideas	Ideophobia
Illness	Nosomaphobia
Imperfection	Atelophobia
Indecisiveness	Decidophobia
Infection	Mysophobia, Molysmophobia
Infinity	Apeirophobia
Injury, physical or emotional	Traumatophobia
Inoculation, injections	Trypanophobia
Insanity	Lyssophobia, Maniaphobia
Insects	Entomophobia
Itching	Acarohobia, Scabiophobia
Jealousy	Zelophobia
Justice	Dikephobia
Knees	Genuphobia
Lakes	Linanophobia
Leprosy	Lerophobia
Lice	Pediculophobia
Light	Photophobia, Phengophobia
Lightning	Astrapophobia, Keraunophobia

Love	Amoraphobia
Machinery	Mechanophobia
Making false statements	Mythophobia
Many things	Polyphobia
Marriage	Gamophobia
Meat	Carnophobia
Men	Andropbobia
Metals	Metallophobia
Meteors	Meterophobia
Mice	Musophobia
Microbes	Bacilliphobia
Mind	Psychophobia
Mirrors	Eisopnophobia
Missiles	Ballistophobia
Moisture	Hygrophobia
Money	Chrometophobia
Monstrosities	Teratophobia
Motion	Kinesophobia
Nagging and ragging	Nagraphobia
Nakedness	Gymnophobia
Names	Nomatophobia
Needles and pins	Belonophobia
Neglect of duty	Parlipophobia
Narrowness	Anginaphobia
New	Neophobia
Night	Nyctophobia, Nyktosophobia
Noise or loud talking	Phonophobia
Novelty	Cainophobia, Neophobia
Ocean	Thalassophobia
Odors	Osmophobia
Odors (body)	Osphresiophobia
Oneself	Autophobia
One thing	Monophobia

Open spaces	Agoraphobia, Cenophobia, Kenophobia
Pain	Algophobia, Odynephobia
Parasites	Parasitophobia, Pluhariophobia
Peanut Butter sticking to roof of mouth	Arachiutyrophobia
People	Anthropophobia
Physical love	Arotophobia
Places	Topophobia
Pleasure	Hedonophobia
Points	Aichurophobia
Poison	Toxiphobia
Poverty	Peniaphobia
Pregnancy	Matensiophobia
Precipices	Cremnophobia
Punishment	Painophobia
Rabies	Lyssophobia
Railways	Siderodromophobia
Rain	Ombrophobia
Responsibility	Hypergiaphobia
Reptiles	Batrachophobia
Ridicule	Katagelophobia
Rivers	Potamophobia
Robbers	Harpaxophobia
Ruin	Atephobia
Russia or things Russian	Russophobia
Rust	Iophobia
Sacred things	Hierophobia
Satan	Satanophobia
School	Scholionophobia, Didaskaleinophobia
Sea	Thakasophobia
Sea swell	Cymophobia

Sex	Genophobia
Sexual intercourse	Coitophobia, Cypridophobia
Shadows	Scioophobia
Sharp objects	Belonophobia
Shock	Hormephobia
Sinning	Peccatophobia
Skin	Dermatophobia
Skin diseases	Dermatosiophobia
Sitting idle	Thaasophobia
Skin of animals	Doraphobia
Sleep	Hypnophobia
Slime	Blennophobia
Smell	Olfactophobia
Smothering	Pnigerophobia
Snakes	Ophidiophobia
Snow	Chionophobia
Society	Anthropophobia
Solitude	Eremophobia
Sound	Akousticophobia
Sourness	Acerophobia
Speaking	Halophobia
Speaking aloud	Phonophobia
Speech	Lalophobia
Speed	Tachophobia
Spiders	Arachmophobia
Spirits	Demonophobia
Stagefright or performing	Topophobia
Standing upright	Stasiphobia
Stars	Siderophobia
Starving	Stervenophobia
Stealing	Cleptophobia
Sullenness	Eremophobia
Stings	Cnidophobia
Stooping	Kyphophobia

Strangers	Xenophobia
String	Linonophobia
Sun	Heliophobia
Surgical operations	Ergasiophobia
Swallowing	Phagophobia
Syphilis	Syphilophobia
Taste	Geumatophobia
Technology	Technophobia
Teeth	Odontophobia
Thirteen at table or number 13	Triskaidekaphobia
Thunder	Keraunophobia, Tonitrophobia
Touching or being touched	Haphephobia
Toxic chemicals in environment	Microchememophobia
Travel	Hodophobia
Trees	Dendrophobia
Trembling	Tremophobia
Tuberculosis	Phihisiophobia
Uncovering the body	Gymnophobia
Vehicles	Amaxophobia, Ochophobia
Venereal disease	Cypridophobia, Venerophobia
Void	Kenophobia
Vomiting	Emetophobia
Walking	Basiphobia, Batophobia
Wasps	Spheksophobia
Water	Hydrophobia
Weakness	Asthenophobia
Wind	Anemophobia
Witches	Wicaphobia
Women	Gynophobia
Words	Logophobia, Verbophobia
Work	Ergasiophobia, Ponophobia
Worms	Helminthophobia
Wounds, physical and emotional	Traumatophobia

| Writing | Graphophobia |
| Young girls | Parthenophobia |

Again, this is only a partial listing.

The Phobia Institute of West Los Angeles has expanded these delineations further and it defines a phobia as "any behavior or feeling that is unacceptable and uncomfortable resulting from conscious or unconscious pictures of the past or projected pictures of the future...or...any thoughts or actions that result in debilitating behavior and decreased optimum performance."

In fact, any sights, sound, memories or thoughts of things or situations which result in negative feelings or undesirable reactions can be considered a Phobia.

Phobic symptoms range from mild anxiety to the extreme phobic reaction of psychological or physical stress. Some commonplace symptoms of phobic disorder can be categorized in three areas: Physiological, Emotional, Social or Work-related.

SOME **PHYSIOLOGICAL (OR PHYSICAL) SYMPTOMS** OF PHOBIC DISORDERS:

Hypertension
Paralyzed limbs
Increased / decreased blood pressure
Wry neck
Increased / decreased heart rate
Palpitations
Temporary blindness
Nausea
Sweaty palms
Vomiting
Sweating
Gas Pains
Muscle tightness and/or spasms
Hyperventilation
Diarrhea
Vertigo

Coronary disease
Headaches - backaches
Respiratory disease
Overeating
Alcohol & Substance abuse
Fainting
Coma

SOME EMOTIONAL SYMPTOMS OF PHOBIC DISORDERS:

Anxiety
Uncertainty
Nervousness
Excessive dependency
Irritability
Hostility
Worrying
Insomnia
Confusion
Hypochondriacal behavior
Sleeplessness
Paranoid reactions
Depression
Disorientation
Impaired thinking
Delusions
Nightmares
Hallucinatory behavior
Hysterics
Panic

SOME **SOCIAL OR WORK RELATED SYMPTOMS** OF PHOBIC DISORDERS:

Forgetfulness
Increase in errors
Low productivity
Job performance anxiety
Unconscious sabotage
Lack of attentiveness
Absenteeism
Boredom
Burn-out
Sexual dysfunction
Communication breakdowns
Divorce
Indecisiveness
Low grades
Alcoholism
Irritability
Substance Abuse

Children and adolescents also suffer from Phobic Disorders such as **School Phobias**.

In fact, phobias in children are so common, that they have been referred to as "childhood neuroses." If you think about it, there are probably very few of us who haven't, at some time in early life, experienced fear of a phobic nature.

Some typical **CHILDHOOD PHOBIAS** include the fear of...

Abandonment
The Dark
Ghosts, witches and demons

Leaving parents
Being Lost
Other kids
Animals
Teachers and authority figures
Illness
Operations
Pain
Hurt

Victims of crime, rape victims, and victims of disaster and trauma, are still another segment of our society who experience Phobic Disorders. There are others who suffer from fears about obesity, alcohol, drugs, smoking, job responsibility, flying, and both personal and business security. Most people at some time or other experience FEAR OF CHANGE (tropophobia).

Finally, every human being undergoes some degree of the following:

LIFE CYCLE PHOBIAS: fear of....

Starting school
Losing children
Puberty
Divorce
Getting out of school
Middle age
Going to work
Growing old
Dating
Getting married
Having children
Disease
Senility
Death & Dying

BIBLIOGRAPHY

Adorno, T.W., *The Authoritarian Personality,* 1975

Ainsworth, Catherine Harris, *American Calendar Customs,* Buffalo, New York, 1979.

Barth, Edna, *Hearts, Cupids, and Red Roses: The Story of the Valentine Symbols*. New York: Clarion Books, 1974.

Barth, Edna, *Shamrocks, Harps, and Shillelaghs: The Story of the St. Patrick's Day Symbols*. New York: Clarion Books, 1977.

Barth, Edna, *Lilies, Rabbits, and Painted Eggs: The Story of the Easter Symbols*. New York: Clarion Books, 1970.

Barth, Edna, *Witches, Pumpkins, and Grinning Ghosts: The Story of Halloween Symbols*. New York: Clarion Books, 1972.

Barth, Edna, *Turkeys, Pilgrims, and Indian Corn: The Story of the Thanksgiving Symbols*. New York: Clarion Books, 1975.

Barth, Edna, *Holly, Reindeer, and Colored Lights: The Story of the Christmas Symbols*. New York: Clarion Books, 1971.

Benson, H., M.D., *The Relaxation Response*, New York: Wm. Morrow & Co., 1975.

Botkin, B. A., *A Treasury of Southern Folklore*. New York, Bonanza Books, 1980.

Browne, Ray, B., *Journal of American Folklore*. (LXXII Vol. No. 94) 1959

Butler, Alban. *Lives of the Saints*. Beverly Hills, California: Benziger, Inc., 1926.

Bulfinch, Thomas, *The Age of Fable or Beauties of Mythology*. New York: The Heritage Press, 1942.

Campbell, Joseph, *The Power of Myth*. New York: Doubleday, 1988.

Cavendish, Richard, Editor, *Man, Myth and Magic*. New York: Marshall Cavendish Corporation, (Vols. 1 through 30), 1970.

Chambers, Robert, editor. *Book of Days*. Detroit: Gale Research Company, 1967 [Repr. of 1886 en.].

Chopra, Deepak, M.D., *Unconditional Life*. New York: Bantam Books, 1991.

Cohen, Hennig and Coffin, Tristram Potter, editors, *The Folklore of Amercan Holidays*. Detroit: Gale Research Inc., 1991.

Column, Padraic, editor. *Treasury of Irish Folklore*. New York: Crown Publishers, Inc., 1967.

Constable, George, Editor, *The Enchanted World*. Vols. on "Ghosts," "Wizards and Witches," and "Fairies and Elves." Chicago, IL: Time Life Books, Inc., 1984.

Conway, D.J., *Celtic Magic*. Minnesota: Llewellyn Publications, 1990.

Conway, D.J., , *Norse Magic*. Minnesota: Llewellyn Publications, 1990.

Croker, Crofton T., and Clifford, Sigerson. *Legends of Kerry*. Dublin, Ireland: The Geraldine Press, 1972.

Cunningham. Scott, *Cunningham's Encyclopedia of Magical Herbs*. St. Paul, MN., Llewellyn Publication, 1991

Cushing, Richard J. *St. Patrick and the Irish*. Boston: Daughters of St. Paul 1963.

Delaney, Mary Murray, *Of Irish Ways*. Minneapolis: Dillon Press, Inc., 1973.

Dilts, Robert, et al., *Neuro-linguistic Programming, Volume I: The Study of The Structure of Subjective Experience*, Santa Cruz, CA: Meta Publications, 1980.

Dossey, Donald E., *Keying: The Power of Positive Feelings*. Outcomes Unlimited Press, Inc. Los Angeles, California, 1988.

Dossey, Donald E., "Through The Briar Patch." (6hr.cassette program) Los Angeles: Outcomes Unlimited Press, Inc., 1987.

Dossey, Donald E., "Predictable Communication Strategies" (4hr. cassette pragram), Los Angeles: Outcomes Unlimited Press, Inc., Los Angeles, CA., 1985.

Dossey, Donald E., *Scared Sick! A Survival Guide for the Age of Anxiety,* Los Angeles: Outcomes Unlimited Press, forthcoming.

Dossey, Donald E., "How to lose the holiday blues," *The California Health Review*, Volume I, No. 3, Burbank,California: Health Review, December/January, 1983.

Dossey, Donald E., "The crisis of everyday life, I & II", *Avenue Magazine*, Encino, CA: Avenue Magazine, August, 1980.

Dossey, Donald E., "Stress and your job," *Avenue Magazine*, Encino, CA: Avenue Magazine, May. 1980.

Dossey, Donald E., "Twenty-first century behavioral medicine", *California Health Review*, Volume I, No. 2, Burbank, CA: Health Review, October/November, 1982.

Dunwich, Gerina., *Wicc Craft; The Book of Herbs, Magick, and Dreams.* New Jersey: A Citadel Press Book. Carol Publishing Group, 1991

Eckman, Paul, M.D., "Body Responds to 'put on' emotions as if real," *Jounal of Psychophysiology, (22: 307-318), CA: 1985.*

Elder, Isabel Hill, *Celt, Druid and Culdee.* Britain: Covenant Publishing Company, 1990.

English, Horace B. and English, Ava Champney, *A Comprehensive Dictionary of Psychological and Psychoanalytical Terms.* New York: David McKay Company, 1958.

Farberow N. L. and Shneidman E.S., editors, *The Cry For Help.* New York: McGraw Hiil, 1961.

Ferguson, Marilyn, editor, *"NIMH Study: 15 Per Cent Mentally Ill In Any Month," Mind/Brain Bulletin,* (Vol.14 No.3), Los Angeles: 1988.

Fox, Arnold, M.D., *The Beverly Hills Medical Diet*. Los Angeles: Chain-Pinkham Books, 1981.

Friedman, A.M., Kaplan, H., and Saduck,J. Editors, *The Comprehensive Textbook of Psychiatry*. (Forth Ed.) New York: Beltmer, Williams & Wilkins, 1985.

Friedman, M., M.D. and Rosenman, R.H., M.D., *The Type A Personality and Your Heart*. New York: Knopf, Inc., 1974.

Gartner, John, Allen, George and Larson, Dave, *Journal of Psychology and Theology*. (19: 6-25), Maryland: 1992.

Godolphin, F. R. B., Editor, *Great Classical Myths*. New York: Random House, 1964.

Grimal, Pierre, Editor, *Larousse World Mythology*. New Jersey: Cartwell Books, 1965.

Haley, Jay, *Strategies of Psychotherapy,* New York: Grune and Statton , 1963.

Hamilton, Edith, *Mythology*. Boston: Little, Brown and Company, 1942.

Hatch, Jane E., editor, *The American Book of Days*. New York: H..W. Wilson, 1991.

Hill, Douglas, *Magic and Superstition,* London: The Hamlyn Publishing Group, Ltd. 1968.

Hillman, James and Ventura, Michael, "Is Therapy Turning Us Into Children?", *New Age Journal*, pp. 60-65, 136-141,May/June 1992.

Horowitz, Rick, *Old Farmer's Almanac*. New Hamphsire: 1987, 1988, 1990, 1991.

Jackson, D.D., "The therapist's personality in the psychotherapy of schizophrenics," *Archives of Neurological Psychiatry*, 74: 292-299, 1955.

Kaplan, Harold, M.D. and Sadock, M.D., editors. *Comprehensive Textbook of Psychiatry/IV*. Maryland: Williams & Wilkins. 1985.

Laing, R.D., *Wisdom, Madness, and Folly*. New York: McGraw-Hill, 1985.

Laing, R.D., *Politics of Experience.* New York: Random House, 1967.

Layne, Lisa and Sinn, Paul, *The Book of Love.* New York: Simon & Schuster, INc. 1984.

Leach, Maria, editor. *Funk & Wagnalls Standard Dictionary of Folklore, Mythology and Legend. New York: Harper* & Row, Publishers, Inc., 1984.

Lisser, Ivar, *Man, God and Magic.* New York: G.P. Putnam's Sons, 1960.

Malbrough, Raymond, *Charms Spells and Formulas.* St. Paul, MN: Llewellyn Publications, 1986.

Magnusson, Magnus, *Hammer of the North.* New York: G.P. Putnam's Sons. 1976

Maple, Eric, *Superstition and the Superstitious.* New York: A. S. Barnes and Co., 1971.

McManus, Seumas. *The Story of the Irish Race.* New York: The Devin-Adair Co., 1921.

McNally, S. J. Robert. *Old Ireland.* New York: Fordham University Press, 1965.

Miller, Alice, *The Drama Of The Gifted Child.* New York: Basic Books, 1981.

Miller, Alice, *For Your Own Good.* New York: Farrar, Straus & Giroux, 1983.

Newall, Venetia, *Man, Myth and Magic* (Vols. No. 27 and 28) 1971

O'Brien, Maire and Conor Cruise, *A Concise History of Ireland.* New York: Beekman House, 1972.

Opie, Iona, and Tatem, Moira, *A Dictionary of Superstitions.* New York: Oxford University Press, 1989.

Padgett, Vernon and Jorgenson, Dale, *Personality and Social Psychology Bulletin* (Vol. 8, No. 4) 1984.

Pilkington, Maya, J., *Alternative Healing and your Health.* New York: Ballantine Books, 1991.

Poinset, M. C., *The Encyclopedia of Occult Sciences*. New York: Tudor Publishing Company, 1939, 1968.

Pollard, Alec, C. and Henderson, Gibson, J., "Social Phobias Found to Affect More Then One of Five," *Jounal of Nervous and Mental Disease,* (176: 343-350), MI: 1989.

Reinstedt, Randall A., *Ghosts, Bandits and Legends*, Monterey: Ghost Towns Publications, 1974

Selye, Hans, M.D., *The Stress of Life*. New York: McGraw Hill, 1976.

Shelton, Ferne, editor, a collection by Helen K. Moore. *Pioneer Superstitions: Old-Timey Signs And Sayings*. North Carolina: Hutcraft, Publisher. 1969.

Spence, Lewis, *An Encylopaedia of Occultism*. New York: University Books,1960.

Szasz, Thomas S., *The Manufacture of Madness*. New York: Harper and Row, 1970.

Tuleja, Tad, *Curious Customs*. New York: Harmony Books, 1987.

USA TODAY, Associated Press poll, February, 26,1992

Weiser, Francis X. *The Holyday Book*. New York: Harcourt, Brace and Company, 1956.

Wood, Garth, *The Myth of Neurosis*. New York: Harper and Row, 1986. Yeats, W. B., editor. *Fairy and Folk Tales of Ireland*. New York: The Macmillan Company, 1973.

Zimmerman, J. E., *Dictionary of Classical Mythology*. New York: Harper and Row, 1964

Index

ABOUT THE AUTHOR:

Behavioral scientist and media personality Dr. Donald Dossey, author of *Keying: The Power of Positive Feelings,* is an internationally acclaimed authority in the treatment of anxieties, phobias and stress and is well known as an entertaining historian folklorian. Dr. Dossey, a former university instructor, founded the Phobia Institute/Stress Management Centers of Southern California. He has been a licensed Marriage, Family and Child Counselor for over 21 years.

Dr. Dossey has tested and adopted a revolutionary new program of telephone home-treatment which has proven to be faster in obtaining results than any other form of one-to-one therapy. He has produced audio cassette Seminar at Home treatment programs that have helped thousands world-wide.

He has hosted his own radio shows "It's Time To Live" and "The Fear Buster." Dr. Dossey is a sought after guest on television and radio broadcasts nationally, as well as programs as far away as Australia and England. His insights have been published in national newspapers and magazines, discussed on hundreds of radio and television shows worldwide including appearances on **CNN, HARD COPY** and **The Oprah Winfrey Show.**

Well known for his humor and rapport with audiences, Dr. Dossey lectures and conducts seminars throughout the world.

Because of his wit and humor, he has been referred to as **"the Will Rogers with a Ph.D."**

NEW HOME SEMINAR CASSETTE PROGRAMS with DR. DONALD DOSSEY

THROUGH THE BRIAR PATCH: In this Home Seminar Program you will learn all of the concrete tools to predictably master Dr. Dossey's "Seven Step Personal Growth Program." Controlling your mind, controlling your feelings and controlling your actions. How to let go of the past and create a future you can chart with ease; and how to wash away any fears, phobias or stress. Six hours. $150.00

PREDICTABLE COMMUNICATION STRATEGIES: A program with NEW communication techniques to better personal relationships, sales and business outcome. Excellent for strengthening relationships. Great for trainers, managers, sales, & counseling practitioners. 4 hours. $95.00

"KEYING" IN SUCCESS: Teaching his world famous Keying technique, Dr. Dossey explains how to eliminate fear and depression, better your health, enrich love and increase financial security. One hour 20 minutes. $15.00

MAKING RESOLUTIONS WORK: After listening to Dr. Dossey being interviewed by radio KBIG's Phil Reed, making New Year's Resolutions work will be easy and fun. 30 Minutes. $10.00

BOOKS

KEYING: THE POWER OF POSITIVE FEELINGS: Overcoming Fears, Phobias and Stress $14.95

HOLIDAY FOLKLORE, PHOBIAS and FUN: Mythical Origins, Scientific Treatments and Superstitious "Cures" $14.95

— — — — — — — — ORDER FORM — — — — — — — —

(Please add $3.75 for shipping and handling for book and $5.00 for shipping and handling audio cassette programs. Californias add 8 3/4% sales tax.)

❑ Payment enclosed   Please charge my   ❑ Visa ❑ MasterCard

Acct. # _____ Exp. Date_____

Signature_____

Please send me_____

Total Amount $_____Telephone (   )_____

Name _____

Address _____

City _____ State_____Zip_____

Send to: Outcomes Unlimited Press,Inc.   Phone orders call:
               1015 Gayley Ave. Ste.#1165   (800) 444-2524 Ext. 2
               Los Angeles, CA. 90024